Special Education

Special Education: What It Is and Why We Need It provides a thorough examination of the basic concept of special education, a discussion of specific exceptionalities, and constructive responses to common criticisms of special education. Whether you're a teacher, school administrator, teacher-educator, or simply interested in the topic, you will learn just *what* special education is, *who* gets it or who *should* get it, and *why* it is necessary. The second edition of this brief yet powerful primer will help you build the foundation of a realistic, rational view of the basic assumptions and knowledge on which special education rests.

James M. Kauffman (Ed.D., University of Kansas) is Professor Emeritus of Education at the Curry School of Education at the University of Virginia. He was the William Clay Parrish Professor of Education from 1992–1994 and the Charles S. Robb Professor of Education 1999–2003. He is a past president of the Council for Children with Behavioral Disorders. He received the Research Award, Council for Exceptional Children in 1994, the Outstanding Leadership Award, Council for Children with Behavioral Disorders in 2002, and the Distinguished Alumni Award from School of Education at the University of Kansas in 2011.

Daniel P. Hallahan (Ph.D., University of Michigan) is Professor Emeritus of Education at the Curry School of Education at the University of Virginia. He was the Charles S. Robb Professor of Education at the University of Virginia's Curry School of Education from 2003–2013. He was the inaugural editor of *Exceptionality* and serves on the editorial boards of *Learning Disabilities Research and Practice*, *Learning Disability Quarterly*, *The Journal of Special Education*, and *Exceptionality*. He is a past president of the Division of Learning Disabilities of CEC and in 2000 received the CEC Career Research Award.

Paige C. Pullen (Ph.D., University of Florida) is Research Professor in the School of Special Education, School Psychology, and Early Childhood Studies as well as the Literacy Initiatives Manager in the Lastinger Center at the University of Florida. She has been principal investigator of many federally funded projects and has authored or coauthored many books, chapters, and articles. She has provided training for both in-service teachers and pediatricians in the USA and also in Zambia and Botswana. She is the editor of the journal *Exceptionality* and serves on the editorial boards of many other journals.

Jeanmarie Badar (Ph.D., University of Virginia) is Instructional Assistant in 2nd grade classrooms in the Charlottesville City Schools. She was a special education teacher for 25 years and served on the faculty of James Madison University. She completed her Master's degree in special education at Kent State University and received her Ph.D. from the University of Virginia. The Badar/Kauffman endowed Conference on Contemporary Issues in Special Education was named in her honor. She is co-author with James Kauffman of another book, *The Scandalous Neglect of Children's Mental Health: What Schools Can Do.*

Special Education

What It Is and Why We Need It

SECOND EDITION

James M. Kauffman,
Daniel P. Hallahan,
Paige C. Pullen, and
Jeanmarie Badar

Routledge
Taylor & Francis Group

NEW YORK AND LONDON

Second edition published 2018
by Routledge
711 Third Avenue, New York, NY 10017

and by Routledge
2 Park Square, Milton Park, Abingdon, Oxon, OX14 4RN

Routledge is an imprint of the Taylor & Francis Group, an informa business

First edition published by Pearson 2004

Library of Congress Cataloging-in-Publication Data
Names: Kauffman, James M.
Title: Special education: what it is and why we need it/James M. Kauffman, Daniel P. Hallahan, Paige Cullen Pullen, Jeanmarie Badar.
Description: New York, NY: Routledge, 2018. | Includes bibliographical references and index.
Identifiers: LCCN 2017054794 (print) | LCCN 2018000322 (ebook) | ISBN 9781315211831 (ebook) | ISBN 9780415792301 (hardback) | ISBN 9780415792318 (pbk.)
Subjects: LCSH: Special education—United States.
Classification: LCC LC3981 (ebook) | LCC LC3981 .K38 2018 (print) | DDC371.9—dc23
LC record available at https://lccn.loc.gov/2017054794

ISBN: 978-0-415-79230-1 (hbk)
ISBN: 978-0-415-79231-8 (pbk)
ISBN: 978-1-315-21183-1 (ebk)

Typeset in Sabon, Frutiger and Stone Sans
Florence Production Ltd, Stoodleigh, Devon, UK

Contents

Preface

Special education is an entirely justifiable idea, but it is often misunderstood or attacked unjustifiably. The concept of special education is essential to universal education in a democratic, benevolent society. In fact, the idea of special education is powerful, which means also that it is open to strong opinions in support and in opposition. The practice of special education is complex. It can be practiced superbly, but often is not. Too often, its practice is disgraceful. The same can be said of general education, which is not automatically a haven for students who need special education and can often be inhospitable to students who cannot thrive there.

Our intention in writing this booklet is to help readers understand both the integrity of the concept of special education and the characteristics of good special education practices. We hope it will help people understand why general education alone is not adequate for some students and cannot be for all.

Intended Audiences and Uses

This booklet is not intended to be a "stand-alone" text for an introductory course in special education. We intend it to be a supplement in which we explain only the most basic problems and features of special education. We see it as a convenient summary that may supplement a special education textbook for an introductory course or an informative supplement to a general education course in which some working knowledge of special education is important. It could also serve as a basic explanation to parents of children and to students in high school who are curious about what special education should be. We realize that we do not address all issues in sufficient detail to satisfy all readers or deal with any issue in the depth that some readers may expect.

Acknowledgements

We are particularly grateful to Alex Masulis, our editor for this book and others, for suggesting that we prepare a second edition of this small book. Alex's foresight in seeing the need for a booklet like this and his guidance through the project have been invaluable.

JMK
DPH
PCP
JB
Charlottesville and Afton, Virginia

chapter 1

How and Why Special Education Is Often Misunderstood

Misunderstanding of special education is common, even though "special education" is a term regularly used in discussion of schooling. Exactly *what* special education is and how it differs from general education, *which students* should get it (and who does or does not), and *why* we should have it are matters that relatively few teachers, parents, school administrators, or those who prepare teachers can explain with much accuracy, consistency, or confidence.

We want you to build a foundation of understanding—a rational and realistic view of the basic knowledge and assumptions that are the bases for special education. Only with such a foundation can anyone sort through the various statements they might hear or read about special education and separate facts from misinformation, truth from fiction. Only then can anyone reasonably weigh proposed changes or reforms and predict their likely outcomes.

After reading this little book you should be able to explain (a) what special education is (and is not), (b) how it differs from the general education of most children, (c) why it is needed, and (d) reasonable outcomes when special education is what it should

W e want you to [have] . . . rational and realistic . . . knowledge and assumptions that are the bases for special education. Only with such a foundation can anyone sort through the various statements they might hear or read about special education and separate facts from misinformation, truth from fiction.

be. We hope this booklet will provide a sound basis for separating fact from fantasy or misconceptions about special education.

We begin by describing some misconceptions about special education and propose more accurate alternatives. We then sketch special education's history in the United States. We explain why special education is such a puzzling matter and touch on problems that simply go with the territory of special education—perpetual issues that demand both decisions and the understanding that points of argument will always remain because there is no definitive, final, not-arguable answer.

Common Misconceptions and More Accurate Concepts

Special education is easily misunderstood. Following are some of the most common misconceptions we have heard or read, along with more accurate statements of fact.[1]

- **Misconception:** Special education is just good education— good teaching of the kind that every student should have. There is nothing really *special* about it.
- **More Accurately:** *Special education* is *not* just good education for typical students *but is instruction that differs significantly from what is effective for typical students*— special in ways we discuss further in a subsequent chapter.
- **Misconception:** Special education is primarily a matter of recognizing that children are diverse in lots of ways and being tolerant and understanding of those who don't learn and behave like most other students.

- **More Accurately**: Teaching anything well requires under-standing of diversity and patience with and understanding of students' differences. However, disability in learning is not like many other types of diversity. *Patience and under-standing are important*; but for teaching students with disabilities, *competence in special instruction is even more important*.
- **Misconception**: Those needing special education are mostly those who have intellectual disabilities (formerly called mental retardation).
- **More Accurately**: Most children with intellectual disabilities do need special education. However, intellectual disability is not the most common disability requiring special education. *Most students with disabilities do not have an intellectual disability*. They are more likely to have learning disabilities and communication disorders.
- **Misconception**: Special education is a place they put kids who are problems or don't fit in, and they're put in special education just so teachers don't have to deal with them.
- **More Accurately**: Most students in special education are not there because they *are* problems but because they *have* problems in learning. Special education is never legitimately —and is not typically—just a way for a teacher to get rid of a student who is a problem. *And special education is not just a place. It is special instruction* that sometimes is best offered in a place other than the general education classroom.
- **Misconception**: Special education is like a "roach motel": A student goes in but does not come out. The fact that so few children exit special education is scandalous.
- **More Accurately**: No one knows how to cure most disabil-ities. Most children who have disabilities require special education and other special supports throughout their school years if they are to make maximum progress. Special education does not typically "fix" disabilities so that they no longer affect students' educational needs or progress. Most students with disabilities have *developmental* problems for which there is no known cure. *The fact that a relatively small number of students receiving special education are eventually found no longer to need it does not mean that*

special education is ineffective for those who continue to need it.

- **Misconception:** Special education prevents students from achieving at a higher level because it offers a watered-down curriculum and low expectations.

- **More Accurately:** Special education should, and often does, help students learn more than they would otherwise. Many students do need a curriculum that is different from that offered to most children. That curriculum is often simplified or addresses needs most students do not have, and expectations should be appropriately high for the individual. It is senseless to teach what students do not need to know or fail to teach what they do need. Also, *having the same expectations for all students may sound good, but is an instructional disaster.*

- **Misconception:** Special education is segregationist. It is a way to accomplish discrimination against children of color, shunting ethnic minorities disproportionately into dead-end programs where their time in school is squandered.

- **More Accurately:** Recent research suggests that African-American children and some other ethnic groups are over-represented in special education compared with their percentage of the general population. However, *children of color are under-represented in special education when compared with otherwise similar Caucasian students.*[2] Children's experiences outside of school may have more to do with their identification as needing special education than their unfair treatment in school. Furthermore, special education is not necessarily a "dead end." General education is and always will be a "dead end" for *some* students when their special educational needs are not identified and served appropriately.

- **Misconception:** Special education is required for *all* children with disabilities because kids with disabilities can't be expected to learn much.

- **More Accurately:** *Some students with disabilities do just fine or excel in general education.* Others fail by any reasonable standard in the general education environment. Special education's purpose is helping students with disabilities learn all they can in school, and for most students with disabilities this means they'll learn a lot. *All* students with disabilities have a right to a free and appropriate education in the least restrictive environment *for them as individuals*. For some students, this means no special education at all. For many, it means special education in the context of general education. For some, it means special education in a separate, special, dedicated environment.

- **Misconception:** Special education is unfair because some kids get educational opportunities or have special legal protections that other kids don't.
- **More Accurately:** *Fairness doesn't mean treating all students the same, regardless of their abilities or disabilities.* Some students have disabilities that don't require any education different from the typical. But other students with disabilities require different treatment at school if they are to be treated fairly. Without special legal protections, these students aren't likely to get what they need. *Fairness in education means that every child receives the teaching he or she needs, whether it's no different, just a little different, or way different from what most kids get.*
- **Misconception:** Special education wouldn't be needed at all if general (regular) education did its job well.
- **More Accurately:** General or regular education has to be designed for students who fall within a range of "typical" or "normal" development. Even if *general education teachers* are doing a superb job, they *can't possibly be expected to deliver the special education that some children with disabilities need.*[3]

Paying attention only to misconceptions about special education might lead someone to conclude that special education is ineffective, misguided, or even malicious and harmful. Although special education has often been poorly practiced and suffered abuses, it is an idea and a set of recommended teaching practices that can make (and often has made) public schooling fairer and more effective than it would be without it.

Historically, it represents the intention to make sure that students with disabilities are not neglected, that they learn all they can, and that they are given a "fair shake" in school.

> aying attention only to misconceptions about special education might lead someone to conclude that special education is ineffective, misguided, or even malicious and harmful. [However,] it ... can make (and often has made) public schooling fairer and more effective than it would be without it.

A Brief History of Special Education in the United States[4]

In the United States, the first formal attempts to provide special education for any children with disabilities began in the nineteenth century. Then, special schools were started for children who were blind or deaf (or both) or had intellectual disabilities. Before these special schools were established, children with these disabilities were kept at home. Usually, they were offered nothing in the way of formal education unless their families could pay the cost of private, highly unusual education. Special schools, often funded by religious groups or other charities if not the state, played a very significant part in the early days of special education. The "universal" public schooling that began in the mid-1800s typically did *not* include students with disabilities.

In the late nineteenth and early twentieth centuries, large metropolitan school districts faced three serious problems: First, large numbers of immigrant children who spoke little or no English; second, large numbers of truant, delinquent, or "wayward" youngsters; and, third, large numbers of children who spoke English and attended school regularly but did not succeed in the standard curriculum with standard teaching procedures. Faced with these problems, some large metropolitan school districts, New York City in particular, instituted special classes for students who were unsuccessful in the typical or general education classes.

To address the first problem, some special classes were designated for "steamer children," recent immigrants who were learning English. Today, we call these children English Language Learners (ELL) or refer to English as a Second Language (ESL). To address the second problem, some special classes were for truant and delinquent students. Today, they would likely be said to have emotional and behavioral disorders (EBD). Still other special classes addressing the third problem were designated as "ungraded" and served "laggards" or "slow" children whose progress was markedly slower than typical. Today, these students would likely be said to have intellectual disabilities (ID) or learning disabilities (LD). In many of the special classes, the emphasis was on vocational skills and work habits as well as basic academics, the assumption being that these students were not going to attend high school or college and should be prepared for work.

At the same time, large metropolitan school districts also found students whose rate of learning was extraordinarily high. Special classes and schools were started for these very high achievers, who today might be called gifted or talented, allowing them to proceed faster and reach advanced levels of performance, sometimes in specific areas such as science or the arts.

A major problem of large city schools in which attendance was required in the early twentieth century was extreme variability among the students to be taught. In fact, an early textbook noted that the problem "is found in the fact of variability among children to be educated."[5] Variability in learning was noted to be the crux of the problem of education again in 1988: "Special education was the solution to the regular educator's thorny problem of how to provide supplemental resources to children in need while not shortchanging other students in the class."[6] In 2015 one of us wrote:

> Even before all children without obvious disabilities were required to attend school (i.e., before school attendance was mandatory in all states for children without disabilities), educators noticed the extreme variability among students. Educators saw the folly in expecting the teacher of a general education class to provide sufficient differentiation in instruction to meet the needs of all students.[7]

By the 1920s, most school districts in the United States had mandatory attendance laws and attempted to accommodate a wide variety of students. However, students with many disabilities, especially if their disabilities were severe, were often left out of school completely. Even many students with relatively mild disabilities were not educated. So, in that era, concerned teachers organized the Council for Exceptional Children, which for a century has been the primary professional association for special educators.

After World War II, special education became much more common in smaller school systems, due in large measure to the action of parents pressing schools for special services. One such organization was the National Association for Retarded Children (later to be called the Association for Retarded Citizens, still later simply the ARC to avoid the "R word").[8]

The first federal legislation involving special education was passed in the 1960s. Although special education expanded greatly in the 1960s, by the early 1970s it was still clear that many children with disabilities were still not receiving special education of any kind. As more students with disabilities were brought into the public education system, the problem of how to respond to the variability in students' learning became more extreme.

In 1975, federal law mandated appropriate education for all children with disabilities (see Martin, 2013). Special education was an invention designed to address the fact of variability among students by reducing it to a reasonably manageable level in a given classroom. And, although special classes were still common, some students were "mainstreamed" for certain activities. "Mainstreaming" (now called "including") students with mild disabilities for part or most of the school day became

> In 1975, federal law mandated appropriate education for all children with disabilities. . . . Special education was an invention designed to address the fact of variability among students by reducing it to a reasonably manageable level in a given classroom.

popular in the 1970s. However, some observers offered cautions that the idea of "mainstreaming" could be abused:

> I am concerned today ... about the pell-mell, and I fear naïve, mad dash to mainstream children, based on our hopes of better things for them. I fear we are failing to develop our approach to mainstreaming with full recognition of the barriers which must be overcome. [. . .] There is a mythical quality to our approach to mainstreaming. It has faddish properties, and my concern is that we do not deceive ourselves because we so earnestly seek to rectify the ills of segregation. We must seek the truth and we must tolerate and welcome the pain that such a careful search will bring to us. It will not be easy in developing mainstreaming, but we cannot sweep the problems under the rug. [. . .] But we must also avoid those well intentioned lies that ignore the weaknesses in a well intentioned system, because we are afraid that exposure will hurt our cause. We should not allow our belief in the promises of mainstreaming to cause us to be silent if we see faults in its application. With the newly recognized rights of children to the education we offer, there must be an equal responsibility to see that those rights are truly fulfilled.[9]

In 1975, a breakthrough federal special education law was passed. It was best known then as Public Law 94-142, after 1990 as the *Individuals with Disabilities Education Act* or IDEA. This law may have been as important for students with disabilities as the 1954 U.S. Supreme Court school desegregation case, *Brown v. Board of Education of Topeka*, was for students of color. However, it is important not to confuse the intent and meaning of these two civil rights laws.[10]

IDEA was enacted in response to advocates for children with disabilities, mainly parents joined by educators, who were unhappy with the extent and types of special education services being offered in schools under state laws. Parents wanted their children with disabilities to receive special education and to be educated appropriately. Many of the unserved children had severe or profound, often multiple, disabilities and had been denied access to any public schooling at all. Others had less severe disabilities but were educated in overly restrictive placements.

The 1975 Public Law 94-142 (the *Education of All Handicapped Children Act*; EAHCA) was a *mandatory* federal law. That is, it *required* that if a state wanted to receive *any* federal education monies, then it had to have a plan to offer special education to *all* children with disabilities (then called handicaps), not just some, and it had to give priority to educating youngsters with the most severe disabilities. The 1975 law and its accompanying regulations were quite complicated, but the most important provisions were quite straightforward.

The most recent revision/reauthorization of the IDEA (as of this writing in 2017) was in 2004, when it actually became the *Individuals with Disabilities Education Improvement Act*, IDEIA, although it's still typically referred to as IDEA. The basic provisions of the law have remained the same since 1975. The most fundamental or basic elements of IDEA are listed, along with the acronyms typically used for them, and explained briefly in Table 1.1.

The first and most fundamental requirement of the law is FAPE, but the other requirements are also important. The CAP has occasionally been confused with services. The law does call for services the student needs as part of the IEP, but it is inaccurate to substitute the concept or the word *services* with that of the concept or word *placement*. The two are different in meaning. LRE has been a particularly controversial provision of the law in the minds and rhetoric of those who advocate full inclusion.

LRE in the law refers to the least restrictive environment in which the particular services the individual student needs can be delivered effectively. Full inclusion proponents maintain that the LRE is always—invariably, for *all* students—the regular or general education classroom. However, the law does not state that, and many proponents of the FAPE and CAP provisions of the law argue that the law neither assumes nor requires the general education placement of all students. The IEP is the methodological part of the law that makes all the others meaningful. Although FAPE, the CAP, and the LRE are critical

Table 1.1 Four Basic Provisions of Federal Special Education Law

Free, Appropriate Public Education (FAPE): Every student with a disability is entitled to an appropriate education at public expense (at no cost to parents or guardians).

Continuum of Alternative Placements (CAP): Placements ranging from separate special schools, hospital schools, and home instruction to special classes, resource rooms, inclusion in regular classes with supplementary services, and all other placement options must be made available to every student with a disability.

Least Restrictive Environment (LRE): Every student with a disability is to be educated in the least restrictive environment that is consistent with his or her educational needs, as close to home as possible, and, insofar as feasible, with students who do not have disabilities. The LRE must be chosen from the CAP and depends on the instructional needs of the student.

Individual Education Program (IEP): Every student with a disability is to have a written, individualized education program that includes statements of the student's present level of performance, objectives of instruction for that student, and the special services to be provided.

Note: Many details and provision of the law and regulations are not included in this table, which includes only the four most basic definitions and core requirements of the law. Other features of the law include communication with parents, assessment and reassessment, and so on.[11]

L RE . . . refers to the least restrictive environment in which the particular services the individual student needs can be delivered effectively. Full inclusion proponents maintain that the LRE is . . . for *all* students—the . . . general education classroom. However, the law does not state that, and . . . the law neither assumes nor requires the general education placement of all students.

T he IEP is the methodological part of the law that makes all the others meaningful. Although FAPE, the CAP, and the LRE are critical parts of the law, they are all dependent on the IEP. Only through planning a program for the individual student with disabilities can the first three provisions of the law be made realities.

parts of the law, they are all dependent on the IEP. Only through planning a program for the individual student with disabilities can the first three provisions of the law be made realities.

When the U.S. Congress enacted the EAHCA in 1975, legislators knew that special education would cost considerably more than general education on a per pupil basis (actually, several times over, on average). When the federal law was passed, Congress stated its expectation that the federal government would pick up 40 percent of the excess cost of educating students with disabilities. However, that federal share of the excess cost has never approached 40 percent.

Attempts to change certain aspects of special education have been constant and repeated since the 1980s. In the mid-1980s, Madeline Will (then Assistant Secretary of Education in the Bureau of Education for the Handicapped) proposed a "regular education initiative" (which became known as the REI). The REI was the first among several attempts to return responsibility for many or most students with disabilities to regular classroom teachers.[12] The REI of the 1980s became the "full inclusion movement" (FIM) of the 1990s. The FIM persists and has become an international movement advocating that all students, regardless of the nature or severity of their disabilities, be included in general education, the same schools, classes curricula, and assessments they would experience if they had no disabilities.[13] The FIM has incorporated aspects of other ideas we discuss in more detail later in this book, including "response to intervention" (RTI), "pay for success" (PFS), a "multi-tiered system of supports" (MTSS), "positive behavioral intervention and supports" (PBIS), and a variety of other approaches or practices.[14] The basic ideas of these various programs or frameworks is to make the IDEA framework more flexible and responsive to students' educational needs. The idea is to prevent the learning and behavior problems defining disability from reaching the point at which placement outside the general education classroom becomes recommended. The intent is to prevent, if possible, identification of the student for special education. The basic notion is to avoid special education completely. In spite of the good intentions and ideas of special educators who promote these various movements and ideas, botched implementation of such ideas as RTI has sometimes been used to delay provision of the services students need, having effects that are the opposite of prevention. And in spite of these "new" ideas or frameworks, the basic requirements of federal special education in late 2017 remain—FAPE, CAP, LRE, and IEP. Proposals to change the law will likely persist based on a variety of rationales.

Contemporary and Perpetual Issues

Some of the controversial issues about special education are both current and perpetual. Universal public education, meaning that all children are required to go to school until they reach a certain age and no child is excluded, always creates controversy, simply because of the vast differences in the abilities of individual students. The controversial issues are difficult to address, and people are bound to differ in their opinions about the best ways to address them. Barbara Bateman, a scholar holding not only a law degree but also a Ph.D. in special education, in the 1990s noted that "who, how, and where" are among the perpetual issues of special education.[15] Among the questions or perpetual issues to which Bateman referred are these:

- *Who* should have the authority to say that a student needs special education? On what basis should they make such a judgment?
- *How* should special education differ from general education? What should be special education's nature, objectives, curricula, and outcomes?

- *Where* should special education occur? To what extent can it be or should it be a part of the general plan for universal public education?
- *Who* should teach exceptional children? What personal characteristics and skills should qualify or disqualify them for the job?
- *How* should teachers be prepared as special educators? Who should train them, and what should special education teachers be expected to do?
- *Where* should special educators practice their profession or craft? With whom must they be prepared to work, and in what contexts should they be expected to function?

Dilemmas of Special Education

Whenever a society attempts to provide truly universal education—public or not—special education presents dilemmas. A dilemma means that a person must choose a lesser "evil" because both choices have a downside. So, no matter what decision is made, there is a trade-off, and the only question is which decision is likely to do the least damage.

Special education presents dilemmas because we can't have things every which way. It's not possible to have education that's the same for all students and yet have special education for some. It isn't feasible to have different education for those at the extremes of knowledge or performance, yet have every student be educated in the same place. So, we're caught with difficult decisions such as the following:

- *Which is a worse mistake in the matter of identifying (or not identifying) an exceptionality* (we use the term *exceptionality*

> Special education presents dilemmas because we can't have things every which way. It's not possible to have education that's the same for all students and yet have special education for some.

here because we are considering both disabilities and particular talents or gifted performance—performance far *above* average): *(a) a false positive or (b) a false negative?* A false positive means falsely identifying a student as having an exceptionality—identifying a student as having an exceptionality and needing special education when the student is actually unexceptional or does not need special education. A false negative means not identifying a student as being exceptional when the student actually is, so the student doesn't get the special education services that he or she should have.

- *Which is a worse consequence of a given student's placement: (a) removing the student from general education to meet his or her needs more adequately in a special class or school or (b) keeping the student in general education where his or her education will not be the best it can be and where he or she will not receive appropriate instruction?* Removal from general education risks the stigma of separation and missing out on the general education curriculum; placement in general education risks the stigma of being different from others and having a curriculum ill-suited to the student's needs. Remember that both special education and general education can be practiced either poorly or very well. Remember that the answer need not, in fact, *should* not be the same for all exceptional students. Remember further that it is impossible to offer all possible educational curricula and methods in the same place and at the same time. So, the question really is this: Which choice do we think carries the least risk and the greatest probability of benefit for the student?

- *Which is a worse scenario for a student with exceptionalities: (a) a teacher with little or no special training and little experience who is teaching a small class or group of students or (b) a teacher with exceptionally good training and a lot of experience who is teaching a large class or group of students?* Of course, the situation could be reversed, and then the choice would be very easy: a teacher with exceptionally good training and experience and a small class or group would be preferable to a poorly trained and inexperienced teacher with a large class or group. In the real world, we know that teachers may be well trained or poorly trained, experienced or inexperienced, have either small or large classes, be assigned to teach special education or general education. We see the aforementioned contrast or choice between (a) and (b) as one that will sometimes have to be made in deciding what is best for a particular student. The choice really is: What do we know about the teacher and his or her assignment, and which teacher will best serve the student? Sometimes, placement decisions depend on judgments of the particular teachers who are available.

- *Which is a worse mistake in assessing a student's ability to learn a particular task or skill: (a) underestimating what a student can accomplish, and therefore failing to teach a student something he or she could learn or (b) overestimating what a student can accomplish, thereby requiring the student to fail repeatedly and squandering time that could have been spent teaching something the student could master?* No foolproof, absolutely accurate, errorless system of assessment has been or can be devised: assessment of a student's capabilities is a matter of experienced human judgment that is less than perfect, and no algorithm yields zero errors. As in the case of identification of exceptionality, the decision could be a false positive (assuming that the student can learn the task when he or she can't) or a false negative (assuming that the student can't learn the task when he or she actually can). The question is really this, for purposes of choosing curriculum or learning goals or expectations: Which kind of error does the least damage to the student?

- *Which is worse: (a) the stigma that goes with being unable to perform like age peers in a general education class and being confronted daily with failure or (b) the stigma that goes with being in a special class where the student is able to perform and make progress in a special curriculum?* The problem of the stigma that goes with being markedly different from age peers is not exclusive to disability (it accompanies giftedness, too[16]), nor is it always clear which stigma will be worse or worst. Furthermore, we must consider the possibilities for leadership and modeling opportunities that may be afforded by placement in a special class or school. We can likely attenuate stigma, but we probably can't legitimately reduce it to zero.

- *Which is a worse curriculum for middle- and secondary-school students with disabilities: (a) a curriculum that is essentially the same as the one provided non-disabled students or (b) a curriculum that emphasizes skills that the student lacks but will need to function in the community?* To deny students with disabilities access to the general education curriculum increases the gap between them and their nondisabled peers in comprehension of core content subjects such as history, English, and science. But focusing on regular academics takes away time needed to train students in life skills, such as time management, basic reading and literacy, self-care, money management, job training, and self-advocacy. The question really is this: What information or skills are most critical for the long-term well-being of the student with disabilities?

These are only examples, certainly not all the dilemmas that are part of special education. Our point is simply that special education often, if not always, involves trade-offs, compromises, choosing the lesser of two or least of several "evils." Having to choose among evils defines a dilemma. Special education is not by any means unique in this respect. In many areas of our lives—medical treatment, deciding to end a marriage, spending money, or flying an airplane, for example–we have to weigh one

Having to choose among evils defines a dilemma. Special education is not by any means unique in this respect. In many areas of our lives—medical treatment, deciding to end a marriage, spending money, or flying an airplane, for example—we have to weigh one anticipated cost or probable negative outcome against another. In many areas of our lives, there are no guarantees, only probabilities, not choices we like to make.

anticipated cost or probable negative outcome against another. In many areas of our lives, there are no guarantees, only probabilities, not choices we like to make.

Perhaps some people understandably want to simplify issues or avoid the most difficult questions about special education by assuming that the answer should be the same in all cases. For example, someone might argue that any question about placement should be answered the same way for all students regardless of their abilities or disabilities or that the exact same expectations should be held for all students. This way of thinking—always the same answer, regardless of students' characteristics—seems egalitarian at first blush. But, to us, it seems to reflect a kind of rigidity, an inflexibility, and unwillingness to come to grips with human exceptionality or a readiness to deny it. The consequence of such thinking is education that is unfair because it is ill-suited to the individual, especially to the individual who is very discrepant from the norm.

Finally, we note that some cases of exceptionality are so obvious as to make the dilemmas we have sketched seem entirely avoidable. The most extreme outliers—those with profound disabilities and those who are child prodigies, for example—have differences in learning that rational people can't deny, and few would deny that such students require extraordinary or special education.

However, the largest number of students are those with less extreme differences, less obvious special needs, those about whom one can argue for either x or y for any given dilemma. The largest number of students for whom special education is an issue consists of students on the borderline between typical and atypical, and their identification is a matter of fallible judgment.[17]

> Some cases of exceptionality are so obvious as to make the dilemmas ... entirely avoidable. [Few would deny that] [t]he most extreme outliers—those with profound disabilities and those who are child prodigies, for example ... require extraordinary or special education.]

That is, they are students who present us with the dilemmas like those we have described, and this is an enduring challenge that we explain further in the next chapter.

Summary

Many misconceptions about special education persist in our society. Historically, special education has been an attempt to increase the fairness of universal public education for exceptional learners (those with special difficulties or extraordinary abilities in learning). Since 1975, federal law (now usually called IDEA) has required schools to provide special education for all children with disabilities who need it. Special education has its perpetual issues, including these questions: *Who* should be identified for special education, and *who* should teach exceptional students? *How* should they be served? *Where* should special education be provided? Special education is not an easy challenge, as it presents difficult dilemmas—difficult choices, none of which is cost-free, risk-free, or perfect.

Box 1.1 Case in point

Here, and in each of the following chapters, we offer a composite case in point (constructed from our experiences) for you to think about. We have chosen to make our examples male and the disability a learning disability simply because male and learning disability are the most common categories in special education. However, we hope you will remember that females and other types of disabilities and giftedness are also represented in special education.

Jimmy is now beginning his sixth-grade year. He has always gotten along well with his classmates and teachers. He has always seemed to try hard to learn. He does acceptable, grade-level work in subjects that require relatively little reading. Last year, when he was in the fifth grade, he was reading on a third-grade level. His parents and his teachers were uncertain whether he needed special education. Both his parents and his teachers thought he might just be lagging a little and that if they helped him more and he worked hard enough he'd catch up and be reading on grade level in a year or two. Maybe tutoring in reading is all he needs, his parents thought, but his teachers said he might need special education. His parents and teachers asked, "Are the hassle, possible stigma, and cost worth the potential benefits of special education? Who will teach him? Where will he go to get this special instruction, and what will he be missing out on in his regular classroom to get the special instruction he needs in reading?"

Notes

1. For misconceptions and facts for each category of disability and many special education issues see Hallahan, Kauffman, and Pullen (2018). For common misconceptions about teaching see Heward (2003) and Kauffman (2015c). For explanation of how special and general education differ, see Pullen and Hallahan (2015) and Zigmond and Kloo (2017).
2. Anastasiou, Morgan, Farkas, and Wiley (2017); Gordon (2017); Morgan, Farkas, Cook, Strassfeld, Hillemeier, Pun, & Schussler (2016), Samuels (2017).
3. Pullen and Hallahan (2015), Zigmond and Kloo (2017).
4. For more detailed comments on the history of special education, see Kauffman (1976, 1981); Kauffman and Landrum (2006); Gerber (2017); Hallahan and Mercer (2002); Hendrick and MacMillan (1989); MacMillan and Hendrick (1993); Mann (1979); Martin (2013); Sarason and Doris (1979).
5. Horn (1924, pp. 6–7).
6. Singer (1988, p. 416).
7. Kauffman (2015b, p. 398).
8. The change to ARC ("the arc," not the A-R-C) is indicative of the negative perception of many labels, including what is sometimes referred to as the (you don't even want to say it) "R word." We find such attempts to be "politically correct" ironic and sad because they work to defeat the very purpose for which they are intended—to portray people with intellectual disability (mental retardation, another avoidance of "the R word") in a positive light rather than assuming there is something shameful about the condition, an attempt to sugarcoat or hide the condition. For further comments on labeling and suggestions for reducing stigma, see Kauffman (2003), Kauffman and Badar (2013).
9. Martin (1974, pp. 151–153).

10. See Martin (2013) for a detailed account of how the breakthrough special education law, P. L. 94-142, EAHCA, was brought about. See Kauffman and Anastasiou (in press); Kauffman and Landrum (2009); Maag, Kauffman, and Simpson (2018) for explanation of how *Brown* and IDEA differ in implications for education.
11. For further discussion of provisions of the law and regulations see Bateman (2007, 2017); Bateman and Linden (2013); Huefner (2006, 2015); Martin (2013); Yell (2015); Yell, Katsiyannis, and Bradley (2017).
12. For discussion of the REI, see especially Lloyd, Repp, and Singh (1991); Singer, 1988; of RtI see Pullen and Kennedy (in press); Kauffman, Badar, and Wiley (in press).
13. For explanation of the FIM, see Fuchs and Fuchs (1994); for additional commentary, see Hornby (2014); Imray and Colley (2017); Kauffman and Hallahan (2005); Kauffman, Ward, and Badar (2016); Warnock (2005).
14. Commentary on MTSS and various plans for inclusion can be found in Anastasiou, Gregory, and Kauffman (in press); Fuchs and Fuchs (1994), Fuchs, Fuchs, and Stecker (2010); Kauffman, Anastasiou, Badar, Travers, and Wiley (2016; Kauffman & Badar (2014b, 2016); Kauffman, Ward, and Badar (2016); Pullen & Kennedy (in press).
15. Bateman (1994).
16. See chapter on learners with special gifts and talents in Hallahan, Kauffman, and Pullen (2018).
17. See Kauffman and Lloyd (2017).

chapter 2

Measurement of Educational Performance

Who needs special education? It all depends on how a student "measures up" against an expectation. We can only answer the question by measuring a student's performance and comparing that measurement with a standard derived from what most students the same age can do. The concept of measurement is fundamental to the concept of special education. In fact, measurement is basic to any societal role or goal. Therefore, it's important to see how educational measurement relates to measurement of other things.

Educational measurement is controversial for several reasons. People may disagree about exactly *what* should be measured as well as *how* it should be measured, even if they agree about the issue of what. Then there are questions of *accuracy*—just how accurate the measurement is. Finally, controversy often swirls around *changes* in whatever is measured. People may disagree about the causes of a change, particularly if the change was observed in students with disabilities or in those who are gifted.

A lot of the misunderstanding of exceptional learners and special education comes from misunderstanding of the role of measurement in education.

A lot of the misunderstanding of exceptional learners and special education comes from misunderstanding of the role of measurement in education.

Perhaps it's easier to understand the measurement of the physical attributes of individuals, such as their height and weight, or of performance in sports. Measurement of intelligence, academic competence, and emotional or behavioral characteristics, for example, are more difficult to understand and accept as valid. Because many of the same principles apply to the measurement of anything, however, we sometimes rely on examples with which people are more familiar.

The Problem of Measurement in Education

Measurement is readily accepted in many parts of our lives, such as sports, science, and medicine, but it is particularly problematic in education. Regardless of the area of our lives or the performance in which we're interested, however, the following questions apply:

- What is to be measured?
- How will it be measured?
- How accurate is the measurement?
- Where does the measurement fall in a statistical distribution?
- What is the meaning of the measurement?
- How should we use the results of measurement?

Besides these, an additional question is critically important in assessing the value of special education:

- What effect does special education have on the learning of the individual who receives it?

The answers to the first five questions are not always obvious when the topic is education. In fact, differing answers to these questions have often sparked controversy and conflict among educators and politicians. The subtleties of educational measurement are many and varied. Some entire textbooks, graduate courses of study, professional conferences, and technical journals are devoted wholly to the topic of educational measurement, and some educators have dedicated their entire professional careers to it. So, there is much to say about this topic, but we will attempt to distill a very broad and complex topic into a few pages of explanation.

What Is to Be Measured?

Both educators and the public at large have many different ideas about just what is most important to measure in education. What should students know or be expected to be able to do at a particular age or grade level? Should *all* students of a particular age or grade know and be able to do the same things? If so, who should decide what those things are? Should the same standards or expectations apply to exceptional students and, if not, then what should we expect and who should make the decision regarding alternative expectations?

These are questions about which emotions run high, and arguments about them can become heated. Measurement has a lot to do with holding schools and teachers accountable for students' learning. Accountability itself is a contentious issue—especially for exceptional learners. Some educators have proposed a "core curriculum"—a standard that presumably is critical for *all* students to meet. But the very idea of a core curriculum for students who aren't exceptional learners is a matter of considerable debate, and the application of such a core to exceptional learners is even more controversial. Regardless of how core standards are created and applied, someone in a school district—parent, teacher, superintendent, or politician—is bound to object. What someone considers key, central, or indispensable knowledge or ability is likely to be related to one's own education and culture.

Much of the controversy about *what* should be taught and *when* it should be taught in any school—and therefore what should be measured—involves history. But, then, one could ask, *whose* history? *Whose* books should be assigned reading? *What* should be taught about those literary works? In science, questions inevitably arise about what students should be taught and be expected to know about scientific methods and principles. Evolution versus creationism is only one example of a scientific matter debated by school boards, teachers, parents, and students. And if these are controversial issues for typical students, they are even more controversial for exceptional learners, most of whom have learning problems and some of whom are educationally advanced.

We are tempted to see the controversies about what to measure as applying mostly to the upper elementary and higher grades and only to certain topics—to more advanced study of history, science, and literature, for example. However, disagreement is also common regarding more basic skills in reading, writing, and calculating. What reading skills are important: letter-sound correspondence or whole-word recognition? Oral or silent reading? Decoding or comprehension? When it comes to writing, what spelling and grammatical constructions should be expected or demanded by what ages? In mathematical calculating, what operations (e.g., addition, subtraction, multiplication, division, fractions . . .) should be taught, and when? What level of precision should be required? Should calculators be allowed? What applications of mathematical principles to everyday problems should be expected? Which is more important, the process of obtaining an answer or the answer itself?

Then there is the matter of social skills and other behavioral characteristics related to school success? How skillful is the student in interacting with peers and authority figures? How long is the student able to sustain attention to schoolwork and other things? How assertive, aggressive, morose, depressed, domineering, self-assured, and/or accepting of others is the student? How do we assess "emotional intelligence" and behavioral acceptability? What standards of conduct should be expected? Should all students, including exceptional learners, be disciplined in the same way for the same offenses? How should we accommodate cultural differences?

The list of controversies about what should be taught to whom and when, and what should be measured, and the criteria for judging performance could all be expanded greatly. You probably see that the controversies are made more complex and are nearly intractable when we consider (a) the age or grade at which we should measure particular skills or knowledge and (b) the range of learners at any given grade or age who should or should not be included in whatever is measured. Some people think that we should not "hurry" children, that we should not have the expectation that nearly all children will read by the age of 6 years, for example. Others believe that if a child is not reading by the age of 6 years then we should be very concerned and take special steps to help the child learn to read.

Discussion about education is made even more confusing by the use and meaning of the word *all*.

Some educators and policy makers use the word *all* (as in "all children should know letter-sound correspondence by the age of _____") but clearly do not consider children with severe disabilities to be a part of that *all*. Others consider the full range of children and want *all* to be interpreted literally—to mean each and every child, regardless of his or her level of ability or disability. The literal meaning of *all* may be emphasized by repeating it frequently (e.g., "all means all") and is probably so used most frequently in appeals for full inclusion of all students with disabilities in general education.[1]

We note also that in some cases people argue that something other than the student's performance is the most important outcome. For example, some people may suggest that the *process* of education is more important than what students can demonstrate they have learned. They may feel that engaging students in hands-on experience, self-directed projects, the process of inquiry, and so on is more important than a test score. We agree that the emotional climate of the classroom and school and the extent to which students are actively engaged in

> D iscussion about education is made even more confusing by the use and meaning of the word *all*.

measurement of educational performance

interesting and self-directed activities are important, but these factors alone are not sufficient to judge the quality of education. Students must also be able to demonstrate what they have learned, sometimes by taking a test.

Others may argue that parental satisfaction or involvement is at least as important as, if not more important than, the student's performance. They may feel that schools must convince parents that what is happening at school is important for their children. We agree that parents should be satisfied with their children's schooling, but we doubt that parental satisfaction is well founded if their children are not learning much at school.

And still others may question why more time is not spent on children's moral or character development. They may argue that the current emphasis on academic standards leaves little room in the curriculum for students' development of morals, ethics, and values. They believe that students must be taught right from wrong or be given precepts for deciding moral issues. We agree that students should learn moral and ethical values, but we don't consider learning such values to be incompatible with learning other content. In fact, we believe that moral and ethical values have adequate meaning only in the context of academic competence.

Understandably, people are often confused about standards—how they are set and who is to meet them. Exceptional learners who need special education raise particular concerns about standards. Many children with disabilities will be able to meet "universal" standards, but some clearly will not. For many gifted children, the typical standards are ridiculously easy, too low to offer any real challenge. For many children with intellectual disabilities, the typical standards are obviously too high.

Deciding *what* to measure for individual students is a matter requiring careful judgment. Deciding what to expect or demand is sometimes very difficult because there is a serious risk of being wrong—choosing to measure knowledge and skills that are somehow inappropriate or trivial for the particular student.

Special education is an attempt to ensure that good judgment is used in the selection of *what* to measure. It represents the desire to make sure that the content of education and the basis for accountability are appropriate for the child's characteristics.

> S pecial education ... is the realization that all students cannot be and should not be expected to learn the same things.

It is the realization that all students cannot be and should not be expected to learn the same things, but that realistic challenges are important. It is the understanding that the student's performance, not something else, is the most important thing to measure.

What Tool(s) Will Be Used for Measuring?

In some lines of work or activity, it's easy to see how we should measure performance. Few people have difficulty understanding the best way to measure how far or how high someone can jump, how fast they can run a certain distance, how much they weigh, how much weight they can lift, or how many points they score in a certain game in a certain sport. Many human characteristics can be measured in a very straightforward, easy-to-understand way. True, one has to consider the specifics of what is being measured (e.g., standing long jump or running long jump; high jump or pole vault) and the particular scale (e.g., meters or feet, kilograms or pounds). But virtually no complaint is lodged about the scale of measurement or the particular tools used to measure.

However, measuring educational achievement and estimating educational potential are anything but straightforward. For a lot of things in education, standardized tests or other standardized instruments are used. When a test or other instrument (e.g., a rating scale or screening device) is "standardized," it is used with a large group so that there is a "normative" group with which someone can make comparisons. The "standardization sample" is a large group used for comparisons with others taking the test so that we may say someone scored about average or very high or low, comparatively speaking.

Some people think standardized tests and other devices are the best tools for measuring most things. Some people also think

measurement of educational performance

almost all standardized devices are bad. One alternative to standardized instruments (tools) is personal judgment of such things as work samples or performances or information obtained through direct observation.

Every way of measuring has certain advantages and disadvantages. Useful measurement is necessary for judging whether special education is "working"—whether it is effective in helping the student, especially in comparison with his or her past performance. Comparisons with norms are important for knowing how well a student is doing compared with others and with "universal" standards. It is important to know how a student is doing in class; how he or she is progressing in instructional materials; and how she or he is getting along in a job, higher education, and community life. The most important considerations for special educators are that (a) multiple tools are used, (b) the right questions are asked, and (c) the tools and questions are appropriate for the individual student whose progress is being assessed.

How Accurate Is the Measurement?

Every measurement contains a margin of error. No measurement contains absolutely no error, or is *absolutely* accurate. Some measurements can be extremely precise, but every measurement is an estimate of a "true" measure, even in tool-making and all physical sciences, even if errors of measurement are infinitesimal.

Measurements that aren't anywhere near absolutely precise can nonetheless be very helpful. Consider some examples from everyday life. A road sign may say the distance to the next city is 5 miles, even though the city limits may actually be

The most important considerations for special educators are that (a) multiple tools are used, (b) the right questions are asked, and (c) the tools and questions are appropriate for the individual student . . .

4.8 or 5.1 miles down the road. A radio announcer might say the temperature is 80 degrees when it's actually 80.5 or 79.7 or even 82. But, in both cases, the information is helpful; the measurement is close enough for most of us.

Of course, the important question is how much error, how much imprecision, how much "slop" in a measure is acceptable before it becomes useless? That all depends on the nature and purpose of the measurement. For making precision tools or judging Olympic sports, measurement may need to be extremely precise. For other measurements, such as weather reports and forecasts, distances between cities reported on maps and road signs, IQ, academic achievement, surveys of public opinion, or psychological well being, for example, a lower level of precision is usually judged acceptable and helpful. Reports of surveys often include a margin of error. In an opinion poll regarding an election, pollsters might say, for example, "We found that voters prefer candidate A over candidate B by 53% to 47%, plus or minus 3%."

A lower level of precision might be acceptable for at least two reasons. First, the tools for measuring some things with great precision might not have been invented. Examples are tests of intelligence and academic achievement and opinion surveys. Second, sometimes an extreme level of precision simply isn't important, even for those who care about the matter. That is, the information is helpful, even though it lacks great precision. One example we've already mentioned is measures of weather (e.g., temperature or rainfall or prediction of either) for typical users of the information.

Some measures of psychological characteristics or educational achievement are frequently misunderstood. The late scientist Stephen Jay Gould described the misunderstanding of measures of intelligence in one of his books, *The Mismeasure of Man*.[2] Gould was not opposed to measuring what we call intelligence, nor did he assume that intelligence can be measured only in meaningless or unhelpful ways. He just objected to the idea that intelligence is a fixed, innate characteristic and is measured with great precision. Another way of saying this is that we shouldn't talk about IQ as though it's a thing or entity that one possesses; instead we should talk about IQ *scores*. For example, we don't refer to someone as having "an achievement"; instead, we talk about a person having "an achievement *score*."

The fact is that achievement test scores and IQ scores are neither extremely accurate nor unchangeable. One argument is that IQ scores merely reflect performance on a kind of achievement test. Even so, standardized tests of achievement and intelligence can be helpful in estimating what a person knows and can be expected to do or learn in the short run.

Tests used in social sciences such as psychology and education all have a *standard error* or estimate of the range within which a student's true score falls. That is, the standard error of a test tells us that the score obtained (let's say, an IQ score of 100) is *probably* accurate within a given range (let's say, + or − 5 points). So, if a person's tested IQ score is found to be 100, and the test has a standard error of 5, then the person's actual IQ score is very likely to be somewhere between 95 and 105. The way a standard error is calculated isn't really important here. The point is simply that for certain tests, we can calculate an *estimate* of the accuracy of the test.

Educators are expected to make educated guesses about students. Measuring education-related things and making educated guesses are parts of special education that can't be avoided or wished away.[3] "Educated" guesses are based on the best available data. Drawing lines to separate one group or category of student from another is required for achieving social justice in education, just as it is in other matters such as sobriety, illness, or financial assistance.

The reason we have testing and other forms of assessment is that they help us make better-informed judgments or guesses, not to rely solely on more subjective judgments. All educators,

> # N
> o . . . evaluation instrument used by special educators is absolutely accurate. [. . .] But . . . refusing to make a judgment . . . ensures that a child's special needs will not be met.

including special educators, are expected to make judgments about students who are not typical in some way, who have *special* needs (that most students don't have). Exceptional learners are at the "fringes" of characteristics relevant to schooling. No test, rating scale, or other evaluation instrument used by special educators is absolutely accurate, and judgments can be wrong, even when informed by the best evidence we have.

But, the reality is that refusing to make a judgment or draw a line merely ensures that a student's special needs will not be met. For special education purposes, the more accurate the measure the better, because the decisions made about a student based on measurement are extremely important. We do not want, nor do we believe it is defensible, to identify a student as needing special education or deny a student special education on the basis of measurement that is very inaccurate. This is one reason we should always use multiple measures in making special education decisions—relying on a single measure or test score increases the risk of being wrong.

The Importance of Statistical Distributions

Measuring something—any kind of measurement—results in a statistical distribution. The distribution always has an average or typical and extremes of high and low. It is always important to consider the extremes as well as the typical–what Stephen Jay Gould referred to as the *full house*, the full spectrum of measures.[4] Special education is concerned with students who fall at the extremes—high or low—on distributions of measurement of educationally relevant things such as tests of achievement, intelligence, and social-emotional behavior. On any given measurement, the cut points that define things like intellectual

measurement of educational performance

disability or giftedness are arbitrary (meaning the choice of a particular cut score could be changed). The cut point may be arbitrary, but it may also be reasonable, just as age required for getting a driver's license or voting or buying alcoholic beverages or retiring, etc. may be reasonable but could be changed.[5]

We have been considering where a student's scores fall on statistical distributions of scores for general populations—how a student's performance compares with that of other students in the general population. However, sometimes it is important to measure how a student's performance changes over time without making any comparisons with how other students perform. We sometimes compare individuals with themselves, but eventually it's important to compare what a student does with what others do who are considered typical. The only way to do this is by comparisons with the statistical distributions we get from measuring a large number of other students the same age. True, every student needs to be seen as an individual, and self-comparisons have a critical role to play in evaluating progress, but no student is an island—a person with no connection to others. Comparisons with a large group of others are ultimately needed to make self-comparisons meaningful.

Special education requires deciding where in a distribution of achievement or behavior we think the criterion should be set for receiving particular services. If an exceptional child is to receive education or any other service that "normal" (typical or average) children do not, then we must choose a line or value (point or place) in the distribution that qualifies the child for that special service. Failure to draw a line simply means that nothing special, extra, or different will be done for the student. It precludes special education or leaves it to whim. Someone could argue that the line or criterion should be higher or lower and still recognize that a line is necessary. However, when someone argues that we should not draw a line at all, then they are suggesting the abandonment of special education, simply because it is impossible to have something special or different without having a line—unless individuals are picked at random or according to whim for special treatment, which makes no sense at all. True, any point we pick on a distribution can be criticized as arbitrary or wrong. Establishing a criterion means taking the risk of choosing a bad one. But not choosing a criterion means being wrong for certain.

What Is the Meaning of an Obtained Measurement?

People often misinterpret measurements, especially in education and psychology. They may misunderstand the meanings of terms like mean (arithmetic average), median (point at which half the scores are higher and half lower; midpoint on a distribution), mode (most frequent score), percentile (point below which a given percent of scores fall), and so on. However, misunderstanding or misrepresentation of the meaning of an individual's score—the obtained measurement—is always possible.

Too often, people misinterpret a particular test score (or obtained measurement) as absolutely accurate or as reflecting something inherent and unchangeable (the late Stephen Jay Gould's main point in *The Mismeasure of Man*).[6] People may also overgeneralize (e.g., conclude that one low test score or one high score applies across the board). Or they may dismiss a test score or observation or other measurement as trivial or meaningless when it is not.

The most critical issue in educational measurement is, of course, what you make of it—the score or other obtained measure. There are no set rules for determining what an obtained measurement means, but all of the matters we have discussed to this point have to be taken into account. There is no substitute for thinking carefully about measurement—how and why the measurement was obtained and how it compares with others' scores when measured the same way.

Special education demands that educators, psychologists, and parents together try to figure out what measures of a child's performance mean. In doing this, the following must be considered: (a) the reliability and importance of the measurement, (b) the child's performance compared with that of other children the same age, (c) the child's trajectory or direction, and (d) the likelihood that the child needs special accommodations, supports, or special instruction because she or he is far above or far below expectations for typical learners.

How Can and Should Special Education Change Performance?

Most people would like to see average educational performance improve. This is not just possible but probable if most students are taught better.[7] But many people seem to want to decrease the discrepancies between high and low scorers—to shrink the variance (dispersion of scores from high to low) so that students become more like one another (i.e., so that students become a more homogeneous group). The only way to make a group of students more homogeneous, though, is to neglect the teaching of the fastest students (so that their progress is slowed) and concentrate attention on improving the performance of the slower students (so that their progress is faster). Or, an alternative would be simply not to include the lowest performers at all in a summary. This is simply a mathematical phenomenon, in which things differing in rate get further apart with time.[8]

You could imagine machines (e.g., cars or airplanes) moving at different speeds (rates), or you could just think about the fact that students differ in the rates they learn particular things. For any given skill or topic, some learners are faster than others. Some are a lot faster than the average speed of learning, and some are a lot slower than average. We may not know why this is so. Some individuals just pick up information or skills a lot faster than others. So, if you start with the normal differences in rate of learning, students get more different from each other with time. That is, they spread out or get more heterogeneous, at least if they receive instruction that is best for them, probably even if they all get the same instruction.

So, how *should* special education change things like the distribution of test scores or measures of achievement? What should be the good effects of special education on the individual student, and how should special education change a distribution? Simply put, it should help lower scorers or slower students not be as low or slow as they would have been otherwise and help higher scorers or faster students score higher or be faster than they would have been otherwise. It's really important to realize that better education for all students makes actual discrepancies or distances between the slowest and fastest larger, not smaller, *especially if it is the most appropriate instruction for each learner.* Education, good or bad, can't make failure or low scorers disappear, nor can it eliminate fast learning.

We should be wary of the comparisons people make in evaluating special education. Some people suggest that special education should be judged successful to the extent that it makes the average for students with disabilities like the average for students without disabilities. This is a clearly unreasonable comparison or expectation. Actually, it is the denial of the nature of exceptionalities.[9]

The only comparison that makes sense in evaluating special education is the difference between what exceptional learners achieve *with* compared with *without* special education. This comparison makes sense for individuals and groups of students with various exceptionalities. Often, however, this comparison is impossible under current federal law in the USA because special education mu*st be provided to every student who is found to have a disability.*

Furthermore, making such a comparison raises ethical problems that aren't easily solved. So, in some ways we're prohibited by law and ethics from finding out whether special education works by doing a true experiment. We often have to be satisfied by comparing neglected groups (those who needed special education but for some reason didn't get it). But such students were not randomly assigned to receive or not receive special education, so the best we can do may be to use a sophisticated statistical design to try to figure out special education's effects.[10] At this point, some studies suggest special education does what

> The only comparison that makes sense in evaluating special education is the difference between what exceptional learners achieve *with* compared with *without* special education ... this comparison is impossible under current federal law ... because special education mu*st be provided to every student who is found to have a disability.*

it is supposed to do—improve performance over what it would have been without special education.

Special education *should* result in the failure of fewer students *by standards that are reasonable for them*. It *should* also improve the performance of individual students over what it would have been otherwise, had they not received special education.

Summary

Measurement in education presents many problems, including what is to be measured, and the accuracy of measurement. Understanding statistical distributions and what a measurement means, given the distribution, is very important. Special education requires thinking about how distributions can and should be changed as well as the effects of instruction on individual learners. Exceptional learners may be compared with themselves (in order to measure their progress), but it's ultimately important to compare their performance with that of others, including typical learners. However, judging special education's effectiveness by comparing the achievement of students with disabilities with that of those without disabilities is unfair and irrational. So is comparing students with special gifts or talents with the typical student. Students who are exceptional should do better with than without special education.

Box 2.1 Case in point

Sixth grader Jimmy's parents agreed to allow testing by a school psychologist to see whether he qualified for special education. The psychologist gave Jimmy a standardized, individual intelligence test and a standardized reading test. She found that Jimmy's IQ was 114, a high average score that suggests he should be reading on grade level. She found that Jimmy's reading level was second grade and that 93 percent of sixth graders did better than he did on this reading test (i.e., he scored in the 7th percentile for his age group). So, it looked to the school psychologist, as well as

Jimmy's teachers and parents, that he qualified for special education and that receiving it would be helpful. No one knows precisely why Jimmy has this problem in reading. He received the same instruction as his classmates in general education, but it was not effective for him. Obviously, his IQ score is not in question as an explanation for his low reading performance.

Notes

1. See, for example, SWIFT schools (2017).
2. Gould (1996b).
3. Kauffman, Anastasiou, and Maag (2016); Kauffman and Lloyd (2017).
4. Gould (1996a).
5. See Kauffman and Lloyd (2017) for further discussion of such statistical realities and their implications for special education.
6. Gould (1996b).
7. See Engelmann (1997); Kauffman (2011).
8. Kauffman (2015b).
9. For example, President George W. Bush's Commission on Excellence in Special Education (2002) stated, "Sadly, few children placed in special education close the achievement gap to a point where they read and learn like their peers" (p. 3) and "The ultimate test of the value of special education is that, once identified, children close the achievement gap with their peers" (p. 4). These statements are obviously at odds with reality (Kauffman, 2004, 2005, 2010; Kauffman & Wiley, 2004).
10. For example, a statistical study showed that students achieved more with than without special education (Hanushek, Kain, & Rivkin, 2002). See also Bateman, Tankersley, and Lloyd (2015); Hornby (2014); Imray and Colley (2017) regarding the value of special education.

chapter 3

The Nature of Educational Disabilities

What is it that separates exceptional learners from others? In Chapter 2, we noted quantitative differences, which may also be accompanied by differences perceived as qualitative—differences that set exceptional individuals apart from those who are typical. In fact, we might say this:

> The study of exceptional learners is the study of *differences*. The exceptional learner is different in some way from the average. In very simple terms, such a person may have problems or special talents in thinking, seeing, hearing, speaking, socializing, or moving. More often than not, he or she has a combination of special abilities and disabilities.[1]

True, special education is also the study of *similarities or commonalities* among learners. It's important to understand that exceptional learners don't differ from the typical *in every way*. Exceptional learners are, in fact, typical in some or even most respects. Although an individual may have disabilities in some specific areas, his or her abilities are at least as important to

> The differences that characterize exceptional learners cannot be denied if students are to be treated fairly. Suggesting that children are "more alike than different" doesn't hide their differences or mean these differences can be ignored. The nature and extent of individual differences are the foundation for defining special education.

recognize. And just because a learner is gifted or talented in one area of performance does not mean that he or she is atypical in every way.

Nevertheless, the differences that characterize exceptional learners cannot be denied if students are to be treated fairly. Suggesting that children are "more alike than different" doesn't hide their differences or mean these differences can be ignored. The nature and extent of individual differences are the foundation for defining special education.

That is, recognizing the existence of particular differences and accommodating them in education are required to achieve fair treatment of students. Educators are called upon to use their judgment about the meaning of various measurements (quantitative data) and qualitative differences that constitute disability and appropriate education. The "first commandment" of special education conforming to federal law is that eligibility decisions must be based on professional judgment, not a cut-and-dried quantitative formula.[2]

Disability is never *simply* a matter of scoring at a certain level on a test or tests. The decision that an individual has a disability requires judgment. However, test scores and other quantitative data may *inform* judgment. Subjective, "clinical" information alone in the vast majority of cases is not enough. Ultimately, a disability requiring special education demands *professional judgment* based on accumulated evidence that a student either (a) needs to learn something other than the standard general education curriculum or (b) needs instruction in the general education curriculum other than that received by students without

the nature of educational disabilities

disabilities, or (c) *both*. Failure to make the judgment—to draw a line or take action that recognizes the difference called a disability—denies the student special education services.

Individuals are different in many ways, some of which are important for their appropriate education. Just because a student has a disability or a special gift or talent does not *necessarily* mean that he or she needs special education. The difference must matter for *educational* purposes if special education is required. Many or most individual differences are not relevant to students' education (e.g., differences in height, weight, parentage, color, family wealth). Some of the differences shown by exceptional children (those with disabilities or special gifts or talents) *are* relevant to education. If their particular educationally relevant differences are not recognized and accommodated, then their education will not be appropriate.

All people, whether children or adults, need affiliation for at least some of the time with others who share important characteristics or preferences with them. This is why we have schools, clubs, and various organizations catering to age groups, ethnic groups, fan clubs, support groups, houses of worship, political parties, and so on. Failure to recognize the need of students to be, at least some of the time, with other students with disabilities like theirs closes the door to development of a supportive disability culture.[3] We are *not* suggesting that exceptional students should always be taught in separate schools or classes. We *are* suggesting that there is potential benefit in congregating students with disabilities or special gifts or talents for some purposes and that educators responsible for teaching such students must consider the full continuum of alternative placements (CAP) in education. The notion that a given placement on that continuum is necessarily inappropriate, evil, and "segregationist" or that another is good for all students because it is nondiscriminatory is a misrepresentation of the meaning of exceptionality in education. The CAP is mandated by legal regulation. It ranges from separate special schools to inclusion in general education in the neighborhood school with supplementary services as needed. It recognizes the need to make decisions about the education of exceptional students on the basis of the educational needs of *individual*s.

the nature of educational disabilities   41

In the following sections of this chapter, we describe general categories of exceptionality in which special education may be needed. We note that although categories may be created, abolished, or renamed in federal or state statutes, all of the exceptionalities we discuss are categories that teachers, psychologists, and others who work with students in schools must recognize. Exceptionality, for special education purposes, may involve any one or any combination of the categories we name, and each has a range of extremeness. Individuals with disabilities may have difficulty in:

- Thinking (cognition) or intellect.
- Learning an academic subject or subjects.
- Focusing and sustaining attention to appropriate things.
- Recognizing and controlling emotions and/or behavior.
- Communicating through the use of speech and/or language.
- Hearing.
- Seeing.
- Moving or maintaining physical well-being.

Some individuals have extreme problems in one of these or disabilities in a combination of them—severe or multiple disabilities.

Multiple disabilities may involve specific brain disorders or dysfunction. These include such specific syndromes (clusters of specific characteristics) as autism spectrum disorders (ASD), traumatic brain injury (TBI), Down syndrome (DS), and a variety of other syndromes that typically entail multiple problems.

Individuals may also be exceptional because they have special gifts or talents, usually in thinking, academics, the arts, sports, or some combination of these. "Twice exceptional" individuals have both a disability (or disabilities) and special gifts or talents.

Three Important Points about Exceptionality

Distinction between Disability and Inability

Every disability is an *in*ability, but not every inability is a *dis*ability. In other words, disability is a subset of inability.

A disability is an inability to do something that most people, with typical maturation, opportunity, and instruction can do. This means taking age, opportunity, and teaching into account. For example, most 6-month-olds cannot walk or talk. They have an inability that is not a disability. However, a 5-year-old who cannot talk or walk has a disability. An adult who can't read doesn't necessarily have a disability. It is a disability, however, if he or she has had appropriate instruction that leads most adults to read and still doesn't read. The inability of a seeing person to see well in the dark is not a disability, nor is the typical adult's inability to lift 300 pounds. The inability of a 7-year-old to run 10 miles is not considered a disability, although the inability to walk at the age of 70 usually is. The point is simply that disability is a significant difference from what we expect most people to be able to do, given their age, opportunities, and instruction.

The same goes for gifts and talents. Most children are not able to read at the age of 3 years. Most are not able to hit a pitched ball at age 2, to play a musical instrument well at age 4 or draw a realistic picture of a human at age 5, and so on. Youngsters are not typically able to do these things even with age-appropriate opportunity and instruction.

All Exceptionalities Are Defined by Continuous Distributions

Another important point about all exceptionalities, whether disabilities or giftedness, is that they represent arbitrary (meaning they can be changed) cut points on continuous statistical distributions.[4] This means they all vary from a little to a lot, with very fine gradations being possible. Moreover, *exceptional* fades into *typical* or *normal* without a distinction that is crystal clear and immovable. True, there are the obvious cases. But even more cases are not obvious because an individual is on the border of a line and it is not really clear on which side of a line he or she belongs (e.g., exceptional or not exceptional; should be said to have mild, moderate, or severe disabilities; has a special gift or does not). But failure to acknowledge that we need a line and have to struggle with which side of that line an individual is

> All exceptionalities ... represent ... cut points on continuous statistical distributions. They vary from a little to a lot, with very fine gradations. ... True, there are the obvious cases. But even more cases are ... on the border of a line ... [F]ailure to acknowledge that we need a line and have to struggle with which side of that line an individual is on ... is a mistake. ... Refusal to draw such lines ... ensures that the needs of students with bona fide disabilities will be denied or addressed inappropriately and ineffectively.

on—or should be judged to be on—is a mistake. Such lines are necessarily part of providing any special service. Lines, like the ones defining such things as poverty, need, abuse, adolescence, or senior citizen are essential. Refusal to draw such lines merely ensures that the needs of students with bona fide disabilities will be denied or addressed inappropriately and ineffectively.

Most Exceptionalities Are Relatively Mild

A third important point is that most exceptionalities are relatively mild, not extreme. The largest category of students receiving special education is that of learning disabilities (LD). Relatively few students receiving special education have severe or multiple disabilities. So, it is common for special educators to speak of high-incidence and low-incidence disabilities.[5] High-incidence disabilities are those that occur most often. Low-incidence disabilities are those that occur relatively infrequently. To a large extent, low-incidence disabilities are those that typically are relatively uncommon accidents of birth, such as blindness, deafness, and deaf-blindness; and high-incidence disabilities are those involving more obvious social judgment, such as intellectual disabilities or emotional and behavioral disorders. The relative *prevalence*, high or low, may depend to a large extent on environmental conditions, awareness, and assessment. For example, an increase in accidents, along with increased awareness and

the nature of educational disabilities

accuracy of assessment, could have a large influence on increased incidence in the category of TBI (traumatic brain injury). We must also guard against assuming that the identification of individuals as having a certain category of disability indicates its incidence in the population. For example, although the actual prevalence of emotional and behavioral disorders (EBD) may be comparatively high (5 percent of the school age population is a very conservative estimate), identification of students with such disorders may be low compared with its actual prevalence (considerably less than 1 percent of the school age population is identified as needing special education because of EBD). In the case of EBD, there appears to be an enormous discrepancy between actual prevalence and percent of the population identified as such, and only the most severe and obvious cases are receiving special education. Although EBD (the terminology now preferred by most professionals in the field, although the federal category remains ED or emotional disturbance) is often considered a mild and high-incidence disability, it seems mischaracterized as such.[6] Nevertheless, it is safe to assume that *most* disabilities are on the milder end of a continuum of severity.

The same observations and reasoning apply to the exceptionalities we call special gifts and talents.

Types of Exceptionality

We next offer brief definitions of exceptionalities that often require special education. A full discussion of the definition of each exceptionality is beyond the scope of this book, as well as detailed discussion of the causes and educational treatment of each.[7] Our purpose here is to describe common exceptionalities and comment briefly on why special education may be required for appropriate education of students in each category.

Intellectual Disability

Definition

Intellectual disability (ID, formerly known as mental retardation or MR) includes significantly below average intellectual ability.

Intellectual ability is usually estimated with a standardized test of intelligence, used to obtain an intelligence quotient or IQ score. However, it is not defined by low intellectual ability alone. ID also refers to substantial limitations in ability to function in everyday circumstances in addition to a low IQ score. It involves impairments in some of the following skill areas: communication, self-care, self-direction, social skills, home health and safety, use of community agencies and services, leisure activities, work, and functional academics. In other words, ID is defined by both low intellectual ability and limitations in skills required for independent living (often called adaptive skills or adaptive behavior). Adaptive behavior is usually measured by a standardized rating scale, for which parents, teachers, and others who know the individual well are asked to rate the individual's performance on a variety of tasks based on their observations.

The cut-off score or criterion for both IQ and adaptive behavior are arbitrary—meaning they can be changed, moved up or down. No definition of ID is free of all criticism. However, nearly everyone agrees that some people need extra support in everyday functioning and that, among the reasons for such special needs, are low intellectual ability and limited adaptive skills. In fact, the American Association for Intellectual and Developmental Disabilities (AAIDD) refers to four levels of support needed: intermittent, limited, extensive, and pervasive. That is, some people with ID need only occasional support. Others need consistent but circumscribed or limited support. And a few need extensive support, involving nearly every type of activity. Pervasive support is demanded by some, as they have very minimal abilities to meet the demands of everyday living. In the relatively recent past, levels of ID were called mild, moderate, severe, and profound. Even longer in the past, three levels were called educable, trainable, and custodial.

We caution here that all of the levels or degrees of ID, not just the general definition, are arbitrary. Recall that there are no big breaks or jumps in what we measure about human abilities. Everything we measure varies from a little to a lot, with very fine gradations. Hence, we must just pick a point at which we draw a line, a cut point, and decide that that point or score is where ID (or other disability) begins. Some cases will be obvious or

the nature of educational disabilities

clear. Others will be very difficult to judge. And this is true not only for ID, but for all other disabilities as well.

Why Special Education May Be Needed

Most people easily see why students with more severe ID (i.e., those who need extensive or pervasive support) need special education. Children and youths with such disabilities clearly have education needs that differ significantly from the educational needs of most students. They are very unlikely to become proficient, even with the most intensive and persistent instruction, in the academic skills that most children master before high school. They obviously need a curriculum focusing on the adaptive skills that will allow them to become as independent as possible, although it is clear that they will need lots of support for the rest of their lives. They are extremely unlikely to receive such instruction from general education teachers.

However, for students with milder levels of ID (those needing only intermittent or limited support) there are often arguments about what disability or disabilities the individual has and what should be done to accommodate him or her. Most of the students who have a mild level of ID will need special instruction if they are to learn basic academics and be prepared for the world of work. Without such special education, it is virtually certain that they will fail to attain the level of academic and social competence they could.

Learning Disability

Definition

Long ago, students with one or more learning disability (LD) were called *minimally brain injured, slow learner, dyslexic, or perceptually disabled.* In the 1960s, LD became the typical designation for this type of exceptionality, although there are still strong advocates of using the term "dyslexia." The category remains very controversial, and some may argue that it is a phantom category–doesn't actually exist, that the identification of LD is fatally flawed, or that far too many students in the

United States are considered to have a LD. Our own view is that LD does indeed exist and that estimates of its over-identification are overblown. We think most of the students identified as having a LD really do have it.

The definition and identification of LD remain matters of great debate. For years, the standard method of determining whether a student has LD relied on measurement of a discrepancy between achievement in at least one academic area (usually measured by a standardized achievement test) and intellectual ability (as measured by a standardized intelligence test). In other words, a student was identified as having LD when he or she failed to learn academics in a particular subject at the expected level, based on IQ.[8] More recently, the focus of identification has been on the student's failure to respond successfully to sound instruction delivered in the general education classroom.[9] In other words, a student would be identified as having LD if he or she does not progress at a similar rate and level as his or her peers when taught using good instruction (i.e., instruction validated by research as effective—often called evidence-based instruction).

Regardless of how LD is identified, we are talking about a situation in which the student's performance in a given academic area is inconsistent with the expectations we have based on other information. That is, there is no reasonable explanation (like ID, mental illness, lack of opportunity, poor teaching, impaired vision or hearing) for the student's failure.

> Regardless of how LD is identified ... the student's performance in a given academic area is inconsistent with ... expectations ... [T]here is no reasonable explanation (like ID, mental illness, lack of opportunity, poor teaching, impaired vision or hearing) for the student's failure. Whether LD is seen as a discrepancy between intelligence and achievement or failure to respond to good instruction, the fact is ... learning is below expectations.

Whether LD is seen as a discrepancy between intelligence and achievement or failure to respond to good instruction, the fact is that the student's learning is below expectations, and there seems to be no explanation other than some kind of brain dysfunction.

Like ID, LD can range from very severe to not terribly far from normal. In fact, LD fades into "normal" or "typical" like any other exceptionality, and its definition is, therefore, arbitrary —requiring careful, informed judgment.

Why Special Education May Be Needed

Students with LD fail, by definition, with the instruction offered in general education, even if that instruction is good and successful with most other students. And if these students do not receive special education, then it is highly predictable that they will continue to fail.

Some students with LD can be taught by special educators in the general education environment. However, those with the most severe levels of LD may need special teaching in a special environment aside from the general education classroom. The reason they may need such special education is that they have very special, persistent difficulties in learning that do not and will not respond to the instruction offered to most students or instruction that is only slightly different or slightly adapted to their special needs.[10]

Attention Deficit-Hyperactivity Disorder

Definition

Attention deficit-hyperactivity disorder (ADHD) is a controversial disability that is not now a separate category in federal special education law. It is most often assumed to be part of the LD category, but also is often a part of the ED or EBD category.[11] Sometimes, students with ADHD are served in the category OHI (Other Health Impaired). The prevailing opinion of experts in the field is that ADHD is most importantly a problem of inhibiting behavior—impulsiveness. Individuals with ADHD can't ignore things most people can. They are easily distracted and can't focus their attention. They may know the proper way to behave but be unable to engage in socially appropriate behavior. They thus often seem "scattered," unfocused, and socially obtuse or maddening because they interrupt or misinterpret others' conversations or activities, forget what most people can remember, or otherwise frustrate and anger others by their fidgeting, distractibility, or "flightiness."

Not all individuals with ADHD are hyperactive, and sometimes they are said to have ADD (Attention Deficit Disorder) because they do not engage in high levels of seemingly meaningless activity. However, the common thread of ADHD is inability to focus and inability to inhibit certain behaviors that are necessary to normal functioning in our society.

ADHD can range from mild to severe. It can also be episodic—be more evident sometimes than others, occur in waves, spells, or episodes. Thus, an individual with ADHD may function well sometimes or in some circumstances, but at other times have extraordinary difficulty. The episodic nature of ADHD confuses some people and convinces them that the individual with ADHD *could* focus attention, *could* behave appropriately but simply *chooses* not to. For example, a student might be able to sustain attention to certain things at home (e.g., TV programs or computer games), yet have great difficulty sustaining attention to academic tasks in school. The attentional requirements of the situations at home and in the classroom are quite different.

> The episodic nature of ADHD confuses some people and convinces them that the individual with ADHD *could* focus attention, *could* behave appropriately but simply *chooses* not to. . . .
> The person with ADHD really does not make a conscious choice to behave inappropriately. the individual's exceptionality is a matter of neurological dysfunction that requires special training and, very possibly, medication.

The person with ADHD really does not make a conscious choice to behave inappropriately. The individual's exceptionality is a matter of neurological dysfunction that requires special training and, very possibly, medication.

Why Special Education May Be Needed

Most students with ADHD drive their teachers, not just themselves and their families and friends, to distraction. They are difficult to manage and teach, especially in a large group. Some excellent teachers, including some general educators with training in what to do for such students, can help such students be successful. However, where and how the instruction of a student with ADHD needs to be atypical, not the usual, depends on the nature and degree of the ADHD. Medications may be helpful for many students, but many students with ADHD require special behavior management and instruction that parents and teachers must be trained to provide.

Emotional and Behavioral Disorders

Definition

As we previously noted, emotional disturbance (ED) is the federal category most professionals now call emotional and behavioral disorders (EBD). The definition of ED or EBD may be the most controversial of all federal categories, harder to define satisfactorily than ID, LD, ADHD, or any of the remaining exceptionalities. The terminology of the field is confusing, but the general idea is that the definition refers to behavior that persistently and significantly disturbs adults and peers. The fact that adults and peers are upset by the individual's behavior does not mean that the problem is merely one of others learning to tolerate it. Students with EBD are outliers in failure to learn social skills and adaptive behavior. Their offensiveness to others may be due to their disregard of social norms, but often this offensiveness is also problematic because it is very discrepant from developmental norms. Their behavior, if uncorrected, means that they will likely have increasing problems in getting

> The prison system is filled with people, men and women, who should have been identified and received services in elementary school for EBD.

along with others. Their emotional problems and deviant or unacceptable behavior are likely to hamper interpersonal relationships as well as the individual's self-understanding, feelings of self-worth, and happiness. Ultimately, their behavior can lead to run-ins with the law for a variety of offenses. The prison system is filled with people, men and women, who should have been identified and received services in elementary school for EBD.

EBD can be exhibited in many different ways. The condition includes many different types of behavior, such as inflated self-image or narcissism as well as inappropriate self-derogation, outrageous bluster, or psychopathic behavior as well as excessive shyness or unreasonable self-blame, extreme literalness, or confabulation (making things up or distorted memory, for example). Behavior may vary along the dimensions of *externalizing* (acting out, usually with aggression) or *internalizing* (acting in, usually associated with depression) or both, with many variations of each dimension being possible.

Some of the students with EBD have conditions usually classified as mental illnesses, such as schizophrenia or bipolar disorder (formerly called manic depression). Bipolar generally signifies mood swings from unnatural elation and extreme activity to depression and low level of activity. EBD also includes obsessions, compulsions, extreme shyness or unwillingness to speak, and so on. In short, EBD may be defined by behavior or emotional responses so different from those of other students the same age, and from cultural or ethnic expectations, that they adversely affect schooling, including academic, social, vocational, or personal skills. Students with EBD exhibit such behavior in multiple settings (e.g., school and home). Their problems are persistent, not temporary. Students with EBD often have other

the nature of educational disabilities

disabilities as well. EBD includes disorders of thinking, speaking, conduct, anxiety, and emotions or affect.[12]

Why Special Education May Be Needed

Students with EBD often do not respond to a school and classroom structure that is conducive to the development of most students. They may require far more structure—teacher monitoring and direction—than typical students. They may need a smaller school or class to be able to function well. They may need more precise and remedial instruction in academic areas, direct and extensive training in social skills that their peers do not need, or other adaptations that are extremely difficult to make in a general education classroom. They may be so disruptive in a general education classroom that they take an inordinate amount of the teacher's time and energy and interfere with the progress of other students. Or, they may be so unresponsive to a general education class that it is extremely difficult or impossible for most teachers to instruct them along with typical students.

Communication Disorders

Definition

Disorders of communication can involve speech or language or both. Speech refers to making vocal sounds and putting them together properly so that the listener can understand what is being said. Language refers to sending and receiving ideas, comprehending and using symbols, the communication of meaning.

Speech includes articulation (making speech sounds), fluency (the rhythm and flow of speech), and voice (vocal quality). Speech therapists may work on articulation to help an individual become more understandable. They may work on fluency to help an individual overcome or adapt to disorders of speech flow (e.g., stuttering). They may work on voice to help a person use pitch, loudness, and pleasing vocal quality to become more socially acceptable or to avoid causing laryngitis or other complications.

Language involves the form, content, and social uses of speech (or other language, such as signing or computer-generated speech). Language therapists may help a student understand and use grammar appropriately, understand the appropriate content of speech, or use language appropriately and effectively in social circumstances.

There are many variations in communication that are not disorders. Many of these variations are dialects related to the individual's geographical region or social or cultural identity. It is important not to confuse dialects, accents, and word choice with speech or language disorders. A communication disorder hampers communication with others, causes embarrassment to the speaker, or draws unnecessary attention within the individual's communication community. That is, a speech/language disorder is a difference from expected communication in the individual's usual social context.

Sometimes communication disorders occur without other disabilities, but they often occur along with other disabilities. In fact, communication disorders tend to be prominent features of some other disabilities, such as ASD (autistic spectrum disorders) and ID (intellectual disabilities). Communication disorders are also sometimes found to be the underlying problem in LD or EBD.

Why Special Education May Be Needed

Communication disorders are among the most complex exceptionalities. It is not feasible to teach all classroom teachers everything they need to know about how to identify, assess, and correct all disorders of communication. That is why we have specialists in disorders of speech and language (SLPs—speech/language pathologists). True, much can be done by general education teachers to address communication problems, particularly when they are advised by a speech-language specialist. A speech-language therapist may do much work in general education. However, some of the work for some students needs to be done in an environment different from the general education classroom.

Some individuals need a communication system other than ordinary speech and language because they have physical

the nature of educational disabilities

disabilities that prevent them from using their natural vocal mechanism to produce speech sounds. Some may need such systems because of autism spectrum disorders (ASD) or other cognitive problems. These students may need augmentative or alternative communication (AAC) systems or devices. They may be able to use these systems or devices in typical social contexts once they are equipped and become proficient with them. However, a specialist may be required to evaluate what the individual needs and provide training in its use.

Deafness and Impaired Hearing

Definition

Hearing acuity can be measured fairly precisely using audiology instruments. It is possible to find out through testing hearing (usually by a specialist called an audiologist) what sound frequencies (pitches) a person can hear at a given level of intensity (decibels or loudness). As is true for most human traits, hearing acuity is continuously distributed statistically (that is, hearing may vary from very acute to absent, with very fine gradations being possible). So, hearing may be very sharp, about average, a little below average, or way below average. For educational purposes, a person who is hard-of-hearing needs a hearing aid to make efficient use of oral language. For educational purposes, someone who is deaf may not have enough residual hearing to process oral language efficiently, even with a hearing aid.

Why Special Education May Be Needed

Normal development of oral language depends on hearing. True, effective communication is possible without speech—through signing (manual communication). It is also true that some teachers in general education classrooms may learn some signs, particularly if a deaf student is in the classroom. However, most of the world is hearing, and most of the world uses oral language for communication.

And virtually all general education teachers and their students don't become proficient enough in signing to make the classroom

> Virtually all general education teachers and their students don't become proficient enough in signing to make the classroom a communication-rich environment, which it needs to be if the student who is deaf is to thrive academically and socially. [...] Thus ... a special classroom or school in which nearly all communication is manual or supplemented by signing is essential to meet their academic and social needs.

a communication-rich environment, which it needs to be if the student who is deaf is to thrive academically and socially.

Thus, for many deaf students a special classroom or school in which nearly all communication is manual or supplemented by signing is essential to meet their academic and social needs. Learning manual communication is, essentially, like learning another language, and one does not become proficient in teaching and using it in the typical oral social context. Having learned to sign does not mean that a student is now easily accommodated in a general education classroom. Communication, including social exchanges, depends on having a language community— others who speak your language fluently. Most people are not fluent and are not likely to become fluent in signing. Hence, students who are deaf and placed in general education classrooms are very likely to remain socially and linguistically isolated. This may be why more than 15 percent of deaf students are educated in separate schools and another 25 percent are taught primarily outside general education classes.[13] Many deaf people and educators of the deaf see special schools as critical to the success of deaf students. For example:

> Rachel Bavister, who taught deaf students in the [Virginia School for the Deaf] for 30 years described it as an incubator for independence, sheltering students just long enough to teach them how to get along in the world. Among her former students, she said, are a professor of clinical psychology and an accountant.

the nature of educational disabilities

"We have deaf staff [who communicate manually] and [hearing] staff who communicate [both orally and manually], so our kids have absolutely no excuse not to grow up to be citizens, hold a job and contribute," Bavister, who is deaf, said in a written interview.[13]

Blindness and Impaired Vision

Definition

Like hearing, visual acuity, too, can be measured fairly precisely with the well-known Snellen chart and other technology-based instruments. It's possible to find out through vision testing by a vision specialist (usually done by or overseen by an optometrist or physician specializing in the eye, an ophthalmologist) how acute a person's vision is and what level of correction is necessary for specific purposes, such as driving, reading, or walking about. Again, as is true for most human traits, visual acuity is statistically continuously distributed and can range from very sharp to absent, with fine gradations possible—better than normal to way below normal or absent completely. For educational purposes, a person with low vision needs extraordinary corrective lenses, special lighting, and/or large print. For educational purposes, some individuals who are legally blind can't use print and must learn Braille for reading and writing. Such individuals also must learn orientation and mobility skills to be independent.

Why Special Education May Be Needed

Most teachers can, with consultation, learn how to accommodate students with low vision in their general education classrooms. Some general education teachers can accommodate students who are blind *if the students have previously learned Braille or other appropriate versions of instructional materials are available and the blind student has learned orientation and mobility skills.*

Blind students can interact socially in ways that children who are deaf can't, because blind students can hear and have oral language. However, their independence and academic progress

F or students with visual impairments, Braille, orientation, and mobility skills are not likely to be learned without instruction by specialists in special classes or schools.

are likely to be stymied unless and until they become proficient in reading and writing Braille and learning how to orient themselves in a physical environment and get around safely in it. For students with visual impairments, Braille, orientation, and mobility skills are not likely to be learned without instruction by specialists in special classes or schools.

Physical Disabilities and Impaired Health

Definition

Physical disabilities involve a very wide range of injuries, diseases, birth anomalies, and chronic conditions that limit a person's ability to perform everyday activities like most individuals. They include such conditions as cerebral palsy, seizure disorders, cystic fibrosis, asthma, limb amputations or anomalies, and other conditions and diseases too numerous to catalog. The main point is that because of some physical condition the individual can't engage in typical activities or do them in the normal or typical way. Some individuals with physical disabilities use wheelchairs or other adaptive devices that help them accomplish ordinary tasks (e.g., crutches, grabbers, special utensils for eating), or prostheses (artificial body parts).

Impaired health may involve any organ system, for example the central nervous system (brain and spinal column), bones, muscles, lungs, digestive system, skin, or circulation. Some physical disabilities involve multiple organ systems. Physical disabilities may also be episodic (occurring sporadically) or progressive (becoming worse and worse, often gradually). They may be acute (a crisis, from which there is usually recovery) or chronic (constant).

the nature of educational disabilities

Why Special Education May Be Needed

Many or most children with physical disabilities alone need little or no special education, as they can be accommodated relatively easily in general education. However, some do need a protective or specialized environment, at least for a time, that is not feasible in a general education classroom. Some are hospitalized frequently and require instruction in the hospital or at home if they are to keep up with their age peers academically.

Additionally, special education may be needed for some children with physical disabilities because they also have intellectual, sensory, or emotional/behavioral problems. Although most students with physical disabilities do not have other disabilities as well, those with some particular kinds of physical disabilities (e.g., cerebral palsy, seizure disorders) are more likely than physically ordinary students to have additional problems such as LD and ID.

Autism Spectrum Disorders

Definition

Autism became a separate category of disability under the Individuals with Disabilities Education Act (IDEA) in 1990. It is now typically discussed under a broader term, "autism spectrum disorder" (ASD). ASD implies a qualitative impairment of social interaction and communication. It also is often characterized by restricted, repetitive, stereotyped patterns of behavior, interests, and activities. Besides autism, ASD includes Asperger syndrome— much like autism in many ways, but milder and usually without significant delays in cognition and language. In short, the main symptoms of Asperger syndrome involve impaired social skills, with some individuals also experiencing abnormal sensory experiences, such as hypersensitivity to sounds. ASD also includes such things as Rett's disorder (normal development to 4 years of age, followed by regression and intellectual disability) and childhood disintegrative disorder (normal development for at least 2 and up to 10 years, followed by significant loss of skills).

Autism is best thought of as a spectrum of disorders that may vary in severity, age of onset, and combination with other

> **A**utism is best thought of as a spectrum of disorders that may vary in severity, age of onset, and combination with other disorders. . . . No single behavior is typical of all cases. . . . ASD is recognized as a brain dysfunction, although no one knows exactly how the brain is affected.

disorders (e.g., ID, specific language delay or anomaly). No single behavior is typical of all cases of ASD, and no single behavior automatically excludes a child from the diagnosis of ASD. ASD is recognized as a brain dysfunction, although no one knows exactly how the brain is affected or the disorder occurs.

Two common notions about ASD have been thoroughly debunked by careful empirical research. One is that vaccinations cause autism. The other is that individuals with autism and other disorders can communicate effectively via a keyboard by using a method called "facilitated communication" or "rapid prompting."[14]

Why Special Education May Be Needed

ASD may require special education for the same reasons we have given in our discussion of ID, EBD, and communication disorders. That is, depending on the individual student, special education may be necessary to address the student's extraordinary cognitive, social, behavioral, and/or communication needs. Some students with ASD are able to function acceptably in general education without special education, but many are not.

Traumatic Brain Injury

Definition

Like ASD, traumatic brain injury (TBI) became a separate category of disability under IDEA in 1990. TBI is brain damage acquired by trauma after a period of normal neurological

the nature of educational disabilities

development. Commonly accepted definitions of TBI specify that (a) the injury to the brain was caused by an external force, (b) the brain injury was not caused by a degenerative or congenital condition, (c) the brain injury results in a diminished or altered state of consciousness, and (4) the brain injury causes neurological or neurobehavioral dysfunction. Most definitions also specify that the injury is followed by impairments in abilities required for school learning and everyday functioning.

TBI has two major subcategories: open and closed. Open TBI involves a penetrating head wound from such causes as a fall, gunshot, assault, vehicular accident, or surgery—the brain has been opened. Closed TBI involves no open head wound but damage caused by internal compression, stretching, or other shearing motion of brain tissue, such as might result from concussion or violent shaking of a child by an older individual or adult.

Why Special Education May Be Needed

TBI presents varied and unique educational problems that often have been poorly understood and mismanaged. The possible effects of TBI include a long list of learning and psychosocial problems, including language difficulties, cognitive (thinking) problems, and EBD. TBI is often "invisible." Like LD, it is something that we are not likely to notice about a person at first. In some cases, an individual with TBI has paralysis or slurred speech or some other indicator of brain injury that is quickly apparent, but in many cases the person with TBI looks just like everyone else and appears at first to behave normally as well. However, students with TBI may need special education for problems in a variety of areas, including thinking, remembering, planning, interpreting and displaying emotions, relearning skills that have been lost, and so on. Many students with TBI simply can't resume their former lives and be successful without extraordinary help from teachers.

A subcategory under TBI that has received increasing attention is chronic traumatic encephalopathy (CTE), a degenerative brain disease caused by repetitive trauma to the brain. CTE may result from one or more severe concussions or several blows to the

> Chronic traumatic encephalopathy (CTE), a degenerative brain disease ... may result from one or more severe concussions or several blows to the head over time that may or may not qualify as 'concussions.' Researchers have concluded that CTE is highly prevalent among former NFL football players. Tragically, CTE has been implicated in the suicides of several high-profile former NFL players, for example, Junior Seau and Alex Hernandez.

head over time that may or may not qualify as "concussions." Researchers have concluded that CTE is highly prevalent among former NFL football players.[15] Tragically, CTE has been implicated in the suicides of several high-profile former NFL players, for example, Junior Seau and Alex Hernandez.

In the case of the latter, as we write this, lawsuits have been filed by Hernandez's family against the NFL and the New England Patriots for being complicit in allowing Hernandez to continue playing although having obvious signs of cognitive impairment from head injuries.

Deaf-Blindness and Other Severe and Multiple Disabilities

Definition

Without going into the technicalities of definitions, we note that some students are both deaf and blind or have multiple, severe disabilities—two or more severe disabilities, such as ID and physical disabilities; EBD, communication disorders, and impaired hearing; deafness, ID, seizures, and EBD. In fact, some disabilities (e.g., cerebral palsy) are typically accompanied by others as well.

Deaf-blindness, although extremely rare, is often recognized today because of Helen Keller, portrayed in the much-acclaimed 1962 Hollywood movie, *The Miracle Worker*. In addition to being the first person with deaf-blindness to achieve a bachelor of arts degree (from Radcliffe), Keller lectured, championed numerous social justice causes, and authored several books, including an autobiography.

Interestingly, although Helen Keller has been highly celebrated, scholars generally acknowledge Laura Bridgman, about 50 years before Keller, as the first person with deaf-blindness who demonstrated that she could be taught to communicate using braille. What celebrity she garnered was brought about by Charles Dickens when he met and wrote about her in his *American Notes*.

Multiple severe disorders are relatively rare—low-incidence. They usually accompany greater severity (of ID, for example) or syndromes that are known to involve brain injury or malformation.

Why Special Education May Be Needed

Students with deaf-blindness and other severe or multiple disabilities have unusually complex educational needs. Most people do not have difficulty understanding why special education is required. Without highly specialized, persistent, carefully controlled instruction, these students are very unlikely to learn the academic, social, and adaptive skills required for independent or assisted living.

Giftedness and Special Talents

Definition

The definition of giftedness is not as easy as it might first appear, and it remains quite controversial. In part, this is true because giftedness is often thought to be defined by IQ, and intelligence testing is itself a matter of controversy. One of the biggest controversies is whether a person has a general intelligence or more specific kinds of intelligence—whether there are multiple intelligences. The field of giftedness is sometimes described as a division between "lumpers" and "splitters."

But, beyond IQ, there is controversy about whether we can anticipate giftedness or identify it only after the fact. Anticipation means making a guess, based on test scores and/or teachers' judgments, that a student is likely or unlikely to demonstrate giftedness. Identification after the fact means that a student already has demonstrated achievement way beyond that of typical students his or her age.

Besides the controversy about when or how to identify gifted and talented students there is disagreement about just what should be measured or included in gifts and talents. Most of us would include performance in academic areas and the arts. But should gifts and talents include athletics? Social leadership? Moral perception? Persistence? Other personal qualities?

Whatever is included or measured, another issue is just how much above average a person must be to be considered gifted or talented and, of course, just who should comprise the comparison group. Should the student be in the highest performing 10 percent, 5 percent, 1 percent, or other specified percent? And should the student be compared with others in the nation, the state, the school district, the school, or some other group? Should the percentage chosen be of all students in an attendance area, or only of those of the student's own gender, social class, or ethnic group?

We do not have definitive answers to such questions, but it does seem clear to us that students who are considered gifted or talented should stand out clearly from the typical in their performance, motivation, and commitment to a particular activity that is highly valued in our society.

Why Special Education May Be Needed

Because ability or performance is any area is continuously distributed statistically, the identification of a cut-point for triggering special education is arbitrary—open to change. Many people in our society do not have much sympathy for gifted students and may, in fact, resent them or assume that if they're so smart or talented they can take care of themselves. However, without access to a curriculum that is challenging to them— whether in math, science, music, or any other area of performance—they are likely to be bored and achieve far less than they could otherwise.

the nature of educational disabilities

M any people in our society do not have much sympathy for gifted students and may, in fact, resent them or assume that if they're so smart or talented they can take care of themselves. However, without access to a curriculum that is challenging to them—whether in math, science, music, or any other area of performance— they are likely to be bored and achieve far less than they could otherwise.

Federal law has never mandated special education for gifted and talented students as it has for students with disabilities, perhaps reflecting our society's antipathy toward giftedness. Certain groups of gifted students have been particularly neglected, including females, students with disabilities, and students from some cultural and ethnic minorities. Regardless of the personal identification of students with special gifts or talents, it is predictable that the greater the discrepancy between their abilities and those of their typical peers, the less likely that their education needs will be met without special education.

Twice Exceptional Individuals

Definition

The definition of twice exceptional is straightforward. Most disabilities do not preclude having an extraordinary ability recognized as a special gift or talent. Someone who has both a disability or disabilities *and* a special gift or talent is considered twice exceptional.

Why Special Education May Be Needed

The need for special education may be obvious because of the nature and severity of the disability and the nature and degree of the gift or talent. We have mentioned the possible need for special education for each category of exceptionality. All those possible educational needs apply as well to those who are twice exceptional.

Why Some Exceptional Students Do *Not* Need Special Education

Not every exceptionality requires special education because (a) some disabilities, such as some physical limitations, are unrelated to education, or the student may be well taught and well managed by a good general education teacher and (b) disabilities, even those related to education, can be so mild or transitory that special education is unnecessary. Special education is only for those students who are significantly and chronically at or beyond the fringes of acceptable educational performance (i.e., are significant outliers in a statistical distribution of adequate behavior) and will not succeed in school unless they receive instruction that most students do not and should not be expected to receive.

Why Prevention of Disabilities Is Often Not Practiced

Nearly everyone agrees with prevention in principle, but few are willing to implement preventive practices. The reasons are many and have been discussed elsewhere.[16] Given the negative attitudes of many people toward special education and lack of understanding of what special education can prevent, however, resistance to the practice of prevention is probably understandable.

> Not every exceptionality requires special education. ... Special education is only for those students who are significantly and chronically at or beyond the fringes of acceptable educational performance ... and will not succeed in school unless they receive instruction that most students do not and should not be expected to receive.

the nature of educational disabilities

Why would people resist preventing disabilities? First, prevention can be practiced at any of three different levels, two of which can't be practiced without labeling. *Primary* prevention means doing the same thing for everyone so that a problem simply doesn't occur. *Secondary* prevention means taking action after a problem occurs to prevent it from getting worse and to reverse a disability if you can. *Tertiary* prevention means managing a disability so well that complications don't occur as well as learning to cope with the disability in the best possible way.

For primary prevention, no label is necessary, as every individual is treated the same—everyone receives (or should receive) the same thing, and kids don't need to be sorted or singled out. An example is vaccination. But for secondary and tertiary prevention, a label of some kind is completely unavoidable. Talking about the problem—calling it something—is necessary. Actually, even primary prevention requires our naming what it is we want to prevent, but we need not say an individual has what it is we don't want to see (measles, for example). We can't prevent things we won't talk about, and once we've seen it we have to say who has it and who doesn't. We can't do secondary or tertiary prevention unless we're willing to sort individuals into those who do and those who don't have the disability. Many people are loath to admit doing this because they don't want to label individuals.

Second, prevention requires anticipation—knowing what is likely to happen next. We can't prevent what we don't anticipate (i.e., *after* something happens, it's too late to prevent it). Many people are loath to anticipate a disability or complications of it, preferring to deal with a problem only after the fact, believing that anticipation somehow causes a problem to occur. In other words, they believe that merely expecting a problem to occur— the expectation itself—will cause something to happen. We do not doubt that expectations can influence performance, but we do also think such occurrences are relatively rare–uncommon enough that it should not deter us from anticipating difficulties.

Third, prevention requires serving more students, serving them at younger ages and earlier in the development of disabilities, and spending more money, at least in the short-term. All of these are absolute necessities if prevention is to be made a reality. But all are also anathema to those who feel special education already serves too many students, costs too much, and is too quickly deemed necessary.

Fourth, prevention requires having more individuals in the "borderline" category, service to more individuals who are less discrepant from typical. That is, it is a mathematical certainty that if problems are caught earlier and at a cut point less discrepant from average we will have to (a) serve a larger number of individuals, (b) have uncertainty about a greater number of students, and (b) risk making more of the errors called false positives (providing services in cases that did not actually need them).[17] It is absolutely certain that serving individuals with less extreme problems or disabilities means serving a greater number of individuals who are right on or very near the cut point for services. Many people think we should be absolutely certain that a student has a disability before he or she is identified as needing special education. However, prevention requires taking action without absolute certainty that a child has a disability, risking being wrong about identification more readily than risking being wrong about nonidentification.

Fifth, prevention requires something extra, not just what we have in place for all students. Even primary prevention demands that something be added or changed, which costs money and requires extra effort. Secondary and tertiary prevention require even more in the way of extras or changes. What should the extra educational things be called? If the extras are called special education, then some people will object, as they consider special education undesirable or stigmatizing.

Not all disabilities can be prevented, but many could be prevented from ever occurring (e.g., through better health and safety practices, genetic counseling, better general education, better child rearing). Many could be addressed early on, preventing them from getting worse or reversing them and improving prognosis by offering special education earlier. Unwillingness to take preventive action inevitably increases the monetary and human costs, although it does save money in the short-term and allows people to avoid confronting unwelcome realities—for a while. As a society, we respond to

> **N**ot all disabilities can be prevented, but ... many could be addressed early on. ... Unwillingness to take preventive action inevitably increases the monetary and human costs, although it does save money in the short-term and allows people to avoid confronting unwelcome realities. ... As a society, we respond to crises once they have occurred, but we do not respond very well to anticipation of problems or to the things we can see leading up to them.

crises once they have occurred, but we do not respond very well to anticipation of problems or to the things we can see leading up to them.

Summary

Students may need special education for a variety of reasons. Chief among these reasons are special difficulties in thinking (cognition); learning an academic subject or subjects (achievement not consistent with cognitive ability); focusing and sustaining attention or being reasonably still and accessible to teaching; recognizing and controlling emotions or behavior; communicating through speech and language; hearing; seeing; moving or maintaining physical well-being; severe and multiple disabilities (extreme disabilities, including several in combination). Students may also need special education because they have extraordinary abilities. The common terms now used for the categorical designation of these exceptionalities are intellectual disability (ID), emotional disturbance (ED) or emotional and behavioral disorders (EBD), communication disorders, hearing impairment and deafness, vision impairment and blindness, physical disabilities or other health impairment (OHI), autistic spectrum disorders (ASD), traumatic brain injury (TBI), multiple and severe disabilities, and gifted and talented. Exceptionalities may occur in any combination. Individuals with both a disability and a special talent or gift are considered twice exceptional. Many of the individuals in these categories need special education, but some do not. Prevention of disabilities seems like a good principle, but efforts to put prevention into practice meet substantial resistance.

Box 3.1 Case in point

The educators in Jimmy's school see his lag in reading ability as obvious, and the lag has been confirmed by testing his reading. The evidence from both observation and testing suggests that Jimmy does not have a general problem in thinking well, because when he is *told* things he makes good sense of them. What seems to cause him particular problems is decoding written language (i.e., automatically, fluently turning letters and words into their associated sounds, what we call reading). So, for the past year he has received special education instruction for one hour each day in a special resource room with a specially trained teacher. The rest of the time, he has been in a general education class, working alongside his peers who don't have a reading disability. But when his regular class has reading, he has gone to the resource room for special instruction in how to associate letters with written words and sounds.

Notes

1. Hallahan, Kauffman, and Pullen (2018, p. 4).
2. Bateman and Linden (2012).
3. Hall (2002).
4. See Kauffman and Lloyd (2017) for elaboration.
5. Even though the popular term is *incidence*; in most cases, *prevalence* is the correct term. The former refers to the number of new cases during a certain period of time (typically, a year), and the latter refers to the number of cases in existence at a certain point in time. With respect to students identified for special education compiled by states and the federal government, the correct term is usually *prevalence*.
6. For a more detailed treatment of each category, see Hallahan, Kauffman, and Pullen (2018).

7. See Forness et al. (2012); Kauffman and Badar (2018); Kauffman and Landrum (2018); Mattison (2014).
8. See Kavale (2002).
9. See Gresham (2002); Vaughn and Fuchs (2003); Spurlock (2017).
10. Hallahan, Lloyd, Kauffman, Weiss, and Martinez (2005).
11. Kauffman and Landrum (2018).
12. See Forness and Knitzer (1992) for discussion of the definition of the Mental health and Special Education Coalition. See Kauffman and Landrum (2018) for more detailed discussion of definition. See Kauffman and Badar (2018) and Sanchez, Comacchio, Poznanski, Gokik, Chou, and Comer (2018) for commentary on the neglect of children's mental health and the role of schools in responding to their needs.
13. U.S. Department of Education (2002).
14. Helderman (2003, p. B7).
15. Centers for Disease Control and Prevention. (2017); Jacobson, Foxx, and Mulick (2016); Mostert (2014); Travers, Tincani, and Lang (2015).
16. Kauffman (1999, 2004, 2014); Kauffman and Landrum, 2018.
17. Kauffman and Lloyd (2017).

chapter 4

The Nature of Special Education

What is special about special education? What makes it different from good general education, or from good teaching by *any* teacher? The answers aren't simple. We might be tempted to think that special and general education are the same if they're both good. However, they are not and should not be the same.[1] Teaching exceptional learners well requires substantially greater precision and persistence, along with differences in some of the dimensions of instruction, such as pacing, number of trials, structure, reinforcement, and so on. This does not mean that special education teachers are better teachers than general education teachers. Just as teaching general education students requires great skill in teaching typical students in larger groups, special education requires great skill in teaching smaller groups and individuals. Special education requires delivering more precise and persistent instruction to exceptional learners, and this is not always possible in the general education classroom.[2]

In this chapter, we discuss the dimensions of special education that make it—or, at least *should* make it special. Special education can, like anything else, be poorly practiced. We conclude the chapter with the observation that *special education's bottom line should be effective instruction of learners at the* extremes of statistical distributions of educationally relevant characteristics.

Special Education: What Is It, Anyway?

Probably we should start with the definition of special education according to the Individuals with Disabilities Education Act (IDEA):

> Special education means specially designed instruction ... to meet the unique needs of a child with a disability. [. . .] Specially designed instruction means adapting, as appropriate to the needs of an eligible child under this part [of the IDEA regulations], the content, methodology, or delivery of instruction. [. . .] To address the unique needs of the child that result from the child's disability.
>
> (Sec. 300.39 Special Education,
> http://idea.ed.gov)

The most salient characteristic of special education is individualized instruction. Without individualization, special education simply doesn't exist.

One of the key players in creating (in 1975) what is now IDEA had this to say about the nature of special education:

> The cornerstone of special education policy ... has been individualization. IDEA was and remains unique in educational policy in that it prescribes no truth in what is

---

The most salient characteristic of special education is individualized instruction. Without individualization, special education simply doesn't exist. . . . Special education is a way of addressing the core problem of variation in achievement and ability in the group of children to be taught.

---

appropriate for [all] children with disabilities. Rather, it provides for a process whereby the individualized educational program (IEP) team that knows the child determines what is appropriate for the child.[3]

Individualization of instruction is demanded by the wide range of types and levels of severity of disabilities and types and levels of gifts and talents. Special education is a way of addressing the core problem of variation in achievement and ability in the group of children to be taught. We think most people with experience in teaching—as well as those who have not taught but think rationally about the nature of teaching and learning—will agree that as the diversity in a group of students in the knowledge, skills, and abilities to be taught increases, the harder the task of teaching that group. Conversely, lowering the diversity of knowledge, skills, and abilities in what needs to be taught makes the job of teaching a group easier. A century ago, special education was seen as a way of addressing the problem of extreme diversity of students' learning-related characteristics for the benefit of both students and their teachers.[4] Special education both allows the individualization for which it stands and makes the task of general education teachers more manageable, thereby benefiting students in general education as well.

Dimensions of Special Education

Special education is not different from general education in its basic operations, but it is different in the application of those operations. Those who contend that special education is something *all* teachers should be prepared to do tend to see teaching as essentially the same, regardless of the students to be taught. There is an element of truth in that suggestion, but it denies both the complexity of teaching and the variability among students. They might consider the absurdity of suggesting the following:

- All surgeons should be prepared to be neurosurgeons.
- All pilots should be trained to fly all planes.
- All builders should be prepared to build skyscrapers as well as houses.

the nature of special education

- All teachers should be able to teach all subjects at all levels.
- All family practice physicians should be cardiologists as well.
- All drivers should be taught to drive all vehicles.
- All drivers of cars should be able to drive all race cars.

In our opinion, good teaching is not simply good teaching, regardless of who the students are. Moreover, subject matter is not all the same, and subject matter is not the only specialization in teaching. Considering disabilities, special education differs from general education in the way it varies along the following dimensions of teaching:[5]

- Explicitness of instruction and the extent to which it is systematic.
- Intensiveness and relentlessness of instruction.
- Pace of instruction.
- Group size.
- Curriculum.
- Giving corrective feedback.
- Duration and frequency of instruction.
- Structure.
- Positive reinforcement.
- Monitoring and assessment.

Of course, these dimensions of teaching are statistically continuously distributed—they can vary from a lot to a little. Thus,

> Special education differs from general education in the way it varies along . . . dimensions of teaching. . . . These dimensions . . . can vary from a lot to a little. Thus, the distinctions between general and special education can be a bit 'fuzzy,' arguable, or uncertain in some cases. . . . Students can be close to or on the line defining exceptionality, and teaching can be near or on the line between general and special. Where to draw the line will always be an issue; not drawing the line simply means that . . . many students . . . won't get the instruction they need.

the distinctions between general and special education can be a bit "fuzzy," arguable, or uncertain in some cases. This doesn't mean that special education is just imaginary any more than exceptionalities are imaginary because they can be very mild or difficult to distinguish from typical development. Students can be close to or on the line defining exceptionality, and teaching can be near or on the line between general and special. Where to draw the line will always be an issue; not drawing the line simply means that whatever the issue is (disability or special education, for example) will be ignored and an important distinction will not be made. In the cases of disability and special education, the result predictably is that many students will be poorly served by the schools. Students won't get the instruction they need.

In the following sections, we discuss the dimensions of education that help us define special education. Keep in mind that differences in special and general education are matters of degree.

Explicitness of Instruction and the Extent to Which It Is Systematic

"Explicit, systematic instruction" is so often mentioned that calling for it in any education is nearly a cliché. Therefore, we describe what *explicit* and *systematic* mean in special education.

Explicit means expressing something clearly and showing clearly and openly what we mean without attempting to hide or mask anything. It is the opposite of hinting at something so that (in this case, students) need to "construct" their own meaning or "discover" an appropriate response. Explicit teaching in special education requires the teacher to explain skills and concepts being taught in a simple, clear, direct manner. When instruction is explicit, the teacher provides a clear explanation or model of the skill or concept. Explicit instruction is quite different from the constructivism or "discovery learning" that has been popular and may sometimes be appropriate in general education.

Systematic means something done according to a fixed plan, and doing this in the most efficient way. In special education,

the nature of special education

*E*xplicit means expressing something clearly and showing clearly and openly what we mean. . . . When instruction is explicit, the teacher provides a clear explanation or model of the skill or concept. Explicit instruction is quite different from the constructivism or 'discovery learning' that has been popular and may sometimes be appropriate in general education.

this may mean following a routine that has been found to be successful in teaching a particular skill or concept. In special education, instruction adheres to a fixed plan for introducing new information—easy skills come before harder ones. Pre-skills needed for a more complex strategy are taught and recognized as essential. In systematic instruction, high-utility skills are taught and practiced before more difficult skills are introduced. In special education, the typical general education complaint of "drill and kill" is replaced by the "drill to thrill" idea because the clear goal is mastery of skills and concepts that typical students learn more easily, without as much drill and practice.

Systematic instruction is structured, so that the teacher arranges instruction in an organized way—in a pattern or system

*S*ystematic means something done according to a fixed plan. . . . In special education, this may mean following a routine that has been found to be successful in teaching a particular skill or concept. In special education, instruction adheres to a fixed plan for introducing new information—easy skills come before harder ones. . . . [T]he typical general education complaint of 'drill and kill' is replaced by the 'drill to thrill' idea because the clear goal is mastery of skills and concepts that typical students learn more easily, without as much drill and practice.

in which efficiency is key. Instruction is presented in a way that is predictable for the student, who knows in advance how the lesson will go.

Intensiveness and Relentlessness of Instruction

Intensive instruction means a lot of effort concentrated on one particular thing so that the objective is to achieve a lot in a short period of time. One goal of special education is to accelerate a student's rate of learning over what it would be otherwise. The objective is to narrow the gap between the learning of the student with disabilities and typical students to the extent possible.

Few people would argue that intensive instruction isn't needed to accelerate learning. Nor would many people argue that intensity of instruction is bad or that schools don't need different levels of it. However, considerable disagreement will be found about *how* to intensify instruction. Intensity becomes a particular concern in tiered instruction, as we will discuss in the next chapter.

Most typical students should experience general education as being intensely demanding. Many do not. Unfortunately, many general education students are not given intense instruction or frequent opportunities to respond. Part of many plans for reform of general education include stepping up the intensity of instruction—increasing the hours that a specific skill (e.g., reading) is taught and increasing the frequency of students' responses to tasks. The school day or school year may be lengthened, the amount of homework may be increased, class time may be used more efficiently (e.g., on-task time may be increased), or some combination of these.

> *Intensive* instruction means a lot of effort concentrated on one particular thing so that the objective is to achieve a lot in a short period of time. One goal of special education is to accelerate a student's rate of learning over what it would be otherwise.

the nature of special education

Regardless of attempts to reform general education by increasing the intensity of instruction for all students, some exceptional children will need greater intensity than can be achieved in the general education classroom if they are to perform as much like typical children as possible. They may need many more than the usual number of trials, more practice and review, a longer period of instruction, a more "fine-grained" curriculum (one with smaller steps or skills broken down further into components) than is necessary for most students, even those who are relatively low performers but are not found to have disabilities.

Learners with special gifts or talents are likely to find the intensity of instruction appropriate for most students of similar chronological age not challenging enough, even if it is "jacked up." Gifted students need something markedly different from the typical education of their age peers if they are to be challenged. They are unlikely to find appropriate challenges in general education typical for their age peers. Usually, they must be grouped with others whose abilities are similar—either with other students who are chronologically older (i.e., they are accelerated or advanced through grades more quickly than their typical age peers) or with age peers who also have extraordinary abilities.

All good teachers give their students repeated trials as needed, review material, and try to teach all of their students well. But there comes a time when any good general education teacher moves on because most or all of the students have learned the concept or skill being taught. Sometimes, depending on the heterogeneity of the class, this means leaving low performers behind (i.e., they have not yet mastered the skill or idea; they have not become competent in the subject matter). It cannot be otherwise in general education, for otherwise the majority of students would be held back—fail to make progress expected of typical students. The greater the press for meeting high bench marks in the curriculum, the more this is true.

Special education teachers give learners with disabilities more trials, opportunities to respond, attention, and instructional time—they are more relentless in their attempts to make sure the student learns.

> Special education teachers give learners with disabilities more trials, opportunities to respond, attention, and instructional time—they are more relentless in their attempts to make sure the student learns.

True, a special education teacher may eventually decide that trying to teach a particular student a given skill is fruitless and turn to teaching something else. However, the tenacity, persistence, and relentlessness of the special education teacher go beyond what can be offered in general education. The special education teacher may try a variety of instructional approaches that the general education teacher either does not know or simply can't implement in the context of teaching a much larger general education class.

Gifted students may find the review and repeated trials that are necessary for typical or slower learners to be a waste of their time. They can advance through material much faster than normal, learning skills and concepts with few trials and mastering concepts with comparatively little review. If their needs aren't accommodated, they are likely to find school a drag, boring. Most teachers of typical students simply can't provide the necessary accommodations for the students, can't differentiate instruction sufficiently to give them what they need.

Pace of Instruction

Pacing or rate of instruction refers to two things: (a) the pace with which a given lesson proceeds (i.e., the speed with which tasks are presented and responses are demanded) and (b) the pace with which a student is led through a body of knowledge (i.e., the speed with which the teacher builds concepts, discriminations, or competencies).

Most students learn well with a typical pace of both types. Some students learn little or nothing unless the teacher alters the pace significantly.

*P*acing . . . refers to . . .: (a) the pace with which a given lesson proceeds . . . and (b) the pace with which . . . the teacher builds concepts, discriminations, or competencies. [. . .] All really good instruction is relatively fast-paced . . . [t]hat is, students are presented tasks at what, *for them*, is a rapid rate. . . . There is little 'down time,' when there is nothing to do. The pace is fast enough that the student doesn't get bored and is challenged, yet slow enough that the student can keep up.

Pace is speed. When you "pace yourself" you do something at a steady rate. Pace is intensified in special education. The teacher maintains a steady, relentless pace, and the speed is based on the ideas of being systematic and helping the student achieve mastery. Teaching follows a set plan and does not proceed to the next step until the student has mastered a particular step in whatever is being taught.

Good instruction is paced at a proper rate for the child's ability to learn whatever is being taught. All really good instruction is relatively fast-paced *for learners with particular characteristics*. That is, students are presented tasks at what, *for them*, is a rapid rate, and they are given frequent opportunities to respond. There is little "down time," when there is nothing to do. The pace is fast enough that the student doesn't get bored and is challenged, yet slow enough that the student can keep up.[6]

One way in which special education is different from general education is that it accommodates both the extremes of students; the ability to respond to instructional tasks and the interaction of instructional rate with content. That is, for some students, the pace at which tasks are presented and responses expected must be altered from the pace appropriate for typical learners. For some atypical students who have great difficulty in learning or responding, the tasks must be presented at a slower rate and the "wait time" that the teacher allows for responding must be longer than that desirable for typical students. For other atypical students who learn more quickly and easily, the rate must be faster than the appropriate speed for most students.

The appropriate rate of instruction is not the same for all students. It may well be about the same for the great majority of students, but for those at the extremes or fringes of performance (either high or low), the rate may need to be altered significantly. If the rate is altered for all students, then those who are typical suffer. If it is not altered, then those at the extremes suffer. The only way to get the rate right is to make accommodations for those at the extremes by grouping them for instruction so that the rate of the lesson matches their abilities.

Thus, special educators must be acutely aware of pacing and know how to alter both the pace of presenting tasks and expecting responses. They must understand the matter of rate or progress through a curriculum. The typical teacher is not taught to do this with great precision—to accommodate the extremes of learner characteristics. Nor is the typical teacher able to make all the necessary accommodations in the context of the general education curriculum without jeopardizing the learning of either exceptional children or those who are more typical.

Group Size

Special education can offer many of its instructional benefits in part because the teacher is responsible for dramatically fewer students at a time than is true in general education. Teaching special education is particularly labor-intensive. It demands more adults per child than does general education. And this is true because special education demands more explicit, systematic, intensive, frequent, and relentless instruction than does general education.

Although it is undoubtedly true that reducing class size dramatically in general education or having two teachers in classes with students who have disabilities may work in some cases, in other cases it is extremely unlikely to mean that all students will be well-taught unless some are taught in a separate setting. Special education is a service, not a place, but the place constrains the kind and effectiveness of the services that can be offered. Smaller groups increase the likely success of instruction

R esearch ... does suggest that homogeneous (in terms of their prior learning or performance) groups of five or fewer offer the best chance for the kind of instruction special education should provide.

because they allow more teacher–pupil interaction, individualization, monitoring, and feedback and decrease distractions (e.g., of noise and movement).

Research on group size does not address all issues. However, it does suggest that homogeneous (in terms of their prior learning or performance) groups of five or fewer offer the best chance for the kind of instruction special education should provide.

Curriculum

Many exceptional students can successfully learn the tasks and ideas that most students learn, although particularly precise teaching (special education) may be required if they are to make progress in what is important for them. The general education curriculum may be inappropriate for some students unless it is very drastically altered or ignored. For some students with disabilities, it doesn't contain important content. For example, orientation and mobility skills and Braille for blind students are not needed by typical students, but these are critical skills for those who are blind. Likewise, most students do not need and cannot be expected to become as proficient in signing as deaf students. Most students do not require the intensive, explicit instruction in social skills that some students with emotional and behavioral disorders should receive. And for some students with severe cognitive impairments, the instruction that typical students receive in government functions and geography is very clearly inconsequential, inappropriate, and nonfunctional. They may need teaching in everyday self-care that is totally inappropriate for typical students the same age.

In short, the general education curriculum may be appropriate for most students with disabilities, but for some it becomes

[**T**]he general education curriculum may be appropriate for most students with disabilities, but for some . . . the *curriculum* they need includes content unneeded by typical students. The "what" of teaching—curriculum—shouldn't be the same for all students.

nonsensical or the curriculum they need includes content unneeded by typical students. The "what" of teaching—curriculum—shouldn't be the same for all students, unless those with disabilities simply aren't considered except as bodies in the classroom or they are excluded from school altogether.

Giving Corrective Feedback

Research strongly suggests that frequent and appropriate corrective feedback is especially important for students with learning disabilities.

Several reasons may contribute to the necessity of such feedback. Frequent errors are an inherent feature of learning disabilities (i.e., a student's making frequent errors in response to instruction is part of the definition of LD). Without correction —being told a response is wrong—a student is likely to make the same mistake(s) again and to do so more frequently. Furthermore, the longer a student goes without being corrected, the more difficult it is to rectify the problem.

Corrective feedback has been defined in different ways, and different kinds of correction have been suggested and researched. Without going into detail about corrective feedback, we can say that the more quickly it is given, the better the results. Also,

Research strongly suggests that frequent and appropriate corrective feedback is especially important for students with learning disabilities.

the nature of special education

the more explicit the corrective feedback, the better. That is, especially for students with disabilities, just saying something is wrong or hinting at the correct answer or expecting the student to discover the correct answer is likely to be unsuccessful. The teacher also needs to tell the student the correct answer.

Corrective feedback is often paired with teacher modeling— the teacher saying or demonstrating what is correct or asking probing questions and supplying the answer if the student does not. In the typical general education classroom, students who make errors are likely to be ignored or humiliated. For those with disabilities, this is particularly unhelpful. In a small group with a teacher specially trained in how to give corrective feedback, the student with disabilities is likely to learn more successfully.

Duration and Frequency of Instruction

Intensity of instruction can be increased by offering instruction more frequently or for longer periods of time. The amount of time in the school day is limited—a finite resource—and it is usually the same for all students. So, decisions have to be made about instructional priorities (e.g., in reading or math). More time may be needed for instruction in a particular subject, meaning there is less time for something else. Students with various disabilities (e.g., learning disabilities) may need more time devoted to a particular subject than typical students.

With the press for better performance of schools and higher levels of tested achievement of all students, the issues become more important for learners with special needs. The expectation that all students will meet state standards and that all students will receive their instruction in general education classes poses difficult problems for both general and special education teachers.

Structure

Structure here refers to such things as (a) the explicitness of rules and expectations, (b) the regularity and predictability of routines, (c) the amount of teacher direction, (d) tolerance for misbehavior or its precursors, and (e) the nature, immediacy, frequency, and explicitness of positive consequences (rewards) for desirable behavior and the nature, immediacy, and dependability of negative consequences (punishment) for unacceptable behavior. Most students do not need the "tightness" or high level of structure that is necessary for some students with disabilities. Most typical students do well without a highly and carefully structured, controlled and controlling learning environment. Many students with disabilities do not.

Typical students usually find a very high level of structure too confining and rigid, and rightfully so because they do not need it to behave and learn well. Some of those with disabilities, however, find such a high level of *structure* comforting or rely on it to get through the day without becoming upset or upsetting others.

To be sure, a given classroom can have a somewhat differentiated structure for different students. But there are limits to the amount of differentiation that teachers and students can manage. A given environment can no more be structured to be appropriate for every possible student than a given commercial retail establishment can meet the needs and desires of every possible customer. Sometimes, the need for structure that is very different from that appropriate for most students can only be provided in a separate setting. Special education teachers have special training in how to structure the learning environment for students who do not respond well to the structure of a good general education classroom.

Some students are highly skilled at structuring their own lives or environments. They seem to have a knack for directing themselves. They are exceptions, not the rule. Most students need a lot of teacher guidance. Some need teachers to control them a great deal, even more than typical students. Getting the

> Some ... with disabilities ... find ... a high level of *structure* comforting or rely on it to get through the day without becoming upset or upsetting others.

the nature of special education

amount of structure right for students requires different kinds of environments for learning, and these can't all be created in the same place at the same time.

Positive Reinforcement

Although punishment, used expertly, may have an important role in teaching and child rearing, the key to a positive and supportive classroom environment—general or special—is positive reinforcement. That is, rewarding desirable behavior and performance is overwhelmingly important. The general education classroom often does not provide sufficient or effective *positive reinforcement* necessary for students with disabilities.[7]

Well-trained special education teachers are skilled in finding and using positive reinforcement to support the learning and behavior of students who have special difficulty in school. These special teachers know that positive reinforcement must be used particularly carefully, and they modulate such reinforcement so that it is effective for the individual student. They know that to be effective positive reinforcement must be immediate, frequent, enthusiastic, include eye contact, include description of exactly what is being reinforced, build students' anticipation of the reward, and that rewards (social and tangible) must be varied.[8]

Unfortunately, the preparation of general education teachers relatively seldom includes explicit instruction in positive behavior management techniques. Many teacher educators in general education are unenthusiastic about, if not actually hostile to, the use of positive reinforcement (rewards) in learning that is essential for the educational progress of most students with disabilities.

> The general education classroom often does not provide sufficient or effective positive reinforcement necessary for students with disabilities.

We recognize that intrinsic reinforcement is important (e.g., a student's feeling good and obtaining gratification from mastery of a task or idea). However, we also know that most students who have difficulty in school need extrinsic motivation to learn all they can, at least initially. Moreover, we consider motivation or reinforcement as being on a continuum from more to less intrinsic or extrinsic. Although more intrinsic reinforcement may work well for many students, more extrinsic consequences or rewards and greater care in the use of extrinsic reinforcement are often required for those with disabilities.

Monitoring and Assessment

All good teachers check frequently on their students' progress. However, it isn't necessary or feasible to monitor and assess the performance of most students as frequently or as closely and precisely as is required for teaching those with disabilities.

Students with disabilities require closer, more careful monitoring than is typical. In a sense, this is like the closer monitoring of medical patients in intensive care than the less close monitoring of those in general hospital care.

Good training of special education teachers includes instruction in how to monitor students' progress daily in the curriculum. This intense level of monitoring is not necessary for typical students, but it is essential for those with special problems in learning. Their progress is often slow, especially in the beginning of their special education, and both they and their teachers need to be aware of progress, even if it is relatively slow. Students with learning problems need such monitoring because more frequent and more accurate feedback is required.

> All good teachers check frequently on their students' progress. However, it isn't necessary or feasible to monitor and assess the performance of most students as frequently or as closely and precisely as is required for teaching those with disabilities.

the nature of special education

Special Education on a Continuum

Special education consists of an extraordinary response to exceptionality, including more sensitive measurement tools. It employs the same dimensions of instruction that all educators use, but it is more intensive, relentless, structured, and goal-directed than general education is, needs to be for typical students, or reasonably can be for all students. Its difference is not in the essential acts that comprise teaching but in the degree to which various aspects of teaching are controlled and the precision with which they are used. It is like the difference between basic piloting skills and stunt flying skills, typical driving of a car and race car driving, general medical skills and those of a specialist. Consequently, a reasonable question regarding the education of any student is this: Just how special is it, and in what ways is it different from the usual? The answer can range from something like "sort of special in structure" to "very special along all dimensions of instruction."

Just as not all students with disabilities need special education, not all students need education that is special to the same degree. The difficult task is matching the degree of specialness to the needs of the student. Our view is that educators and parents very often underestimate the degree of specialness that is needed.

One of the difficulties in making special education truly special along any dimension is the constraints of a particular place (physical location) on instruction. As we and others have noted elsewhere, it is not feasible to offer all types of instruction in the same place and at the same time.

The degree of specialness possible seems to depend on three primary factors: (a) a teacher who has appropriate special training and is truly expert in implementing teaching procedures with extraordinary precision, (b) a small and relatively homogeneous group of students, and (c) a place in which teacher and students can work without undue interference or demands from others and in which their work does not compete with or impede the education of other students. Researcher and teacher educator Naomi Zigmond observed:

> Special education was once worth receiving; it could be again. In many schools, it is not now. Here is where

practitioners, policy makers, advocates, and researchers in special education need to focus—on defining the nature of special education and the competencies of the teachers who will deliver it.[9]

Before the passage of federal special education law in 1975 (now known as IDEA), the only educational option for many students with disabilities and their parents was a self-contained special classroom or special school. Now, unfortunately, in many places the only option available for many students is the regular classroom or a special school. Even when full-time placement in the general education classroom is accompanied by having a special educator consult with, or even co-teach with the general educator, this can end up being an inadequate version of special education, a "sort of" special education. Too often, the student with disabilities is left with a classroom aide, often minimally trained, as the major "support" in general education. Movement toward full inclusion and consultation between special and general education teachers rather than direct service to exceptional learners by special educators can come at the expense of students with disabilities. The focus on specialized instruction and the intention to train expert teachers in how to deliver such instruction have been neglected. The improvement of special education—making it more reliably what it should be—awaits the rediscovery of such focus and intention.

Special Education's Bottom Line

Special education exists for the primary purpose of providing better instruction to students at the extremes of statistical distributions of school achievement.

Special education exists for the primary purpose of providing better instruction to students at the extremes of statistical distributions of school achievement.

Assessment, placement, and every other aspect of special education must serve the primary purpose of better instruction of exceptional students. If special education fails in this purpose, then it is derelict, regardless of how it is structured.

We do not mean to promote the view that special educators should focus on academics to the exclusion of everything else. Fostering or demanding such an exclusive focus would be perverse. Our point is simply that if special educators do not teach as well as possible, then they have failed in their primary mission, regardless of how kind, sensitive, caring, or collaborative they might be. They could fail because all they teach is academics and nothing else. But if they do not teach what their students need most to learn, then all of the other things they may offer can't make them competent special educators. We quote Naomi Zigmond again:

> General education cannot imagine focusing intensively on individual students to the extent that different instructional activities for different students are being implemented at the same time. This is simply impractical in a classroom of 25 to 35 students. Moreover, special education's most basic article of faith, that instruction must be individualized to be truly effective, is rarely contemplated, let alone observed in most general education classrooms. Mainstream teachers must consider the good of the group and the extent to which the learning activities they present maintain classroom flow, orderliness, and cooperation. In addition, they generally formulate teaching plans that result in a productive learning environment for 90% or more of their students. General education settings are best for learning what most students need to learn.

For many of the remaining 10% of students, however, a different orientation will probably be needed. These students need to learn something different because they are clearly not learning what everyone else is learning. Interventions that might be effective for this group of students require a considerable investment of time and effort, as well as extensive support.[10]

The differences between general and special education remain a matter of great controversy, as does the idea that general education should become so powerful, multi-purposed, differentiated, and welcoming that it is made appropriate for all children, regardless of how low or high their intellectual capability or performance and regardless of any kind of disability they might have. That remains an unfulfilled promise, as does special education. In part, that might be because special education is not designed to provide equal opportunities in the sense of being in the same place at the same time as other students or getting the same instruction as students without disabilities. Instead, it is about giving *unequal* opportunities to exceptional individuals by tailoring instruction to their special individual needs. As Naomi Zigmond and her colleague Amanda Kloo put it,

> special education remains a promise unfulfilled. In the embrace of "normalization" and "inclusion," legislators, school leaders, and parents have focused on ensuring *equal* educational opportunity, but the promise of special education was *unequal* opportunities, special opportunities, different and more appropriate opportunities, tailored opportunities, individualized opportunities. Parents, legislators, and teachers themselves complain that general education teachers are not equipped to meet the educational needs of students with disabilities.[11]

Summary

Although good general education is demanding, special education requires greater control and precision along several dimensions of instruction: explicitness, systematicness, intensiveness, relentlessness, pace, group size, curriculum, corrective feedback, duration, frequency, structure, reinforcement, monitoring, and assessment. Because all of these dimensions of teaching can vary from a little to a lot, education can differ in the degree of specialness, from sort of to very special. Ultimately, special education is only worthwhile if it improves instruction for students at the extremes of performance, low or high.

Box 4.1 Case in point

In his resource room, Jimmy was taught by a special education teacher who knew that he needed reading instruction in decoding words. The teacher had a relatively low case load and was able to spend an entire hour each day working with Jimmy in a small group of students (five) who were about the same age and had similar reading problems. Jimmy was given instruction that focused on decoding, demanded frequent responses from him, provided immediate feedback, and gave him practice in using his skills in reading interesting material on his own reading level. The teacher also maintained daily records of Jimmy's progress and kept his parents and general education teacher informed of how he was doing.

Notes

1. Zigmond and Kloo (2017).
2. See Cook and Schirmer (2006); Fuchs and Fuchs (1995); Kauffman (2015d); Pullen and Hallahan (2015); Zigmond (2003). See also Heward (2003) for discussion of specious arguments about teaching and Silvestri and Heward (2016) for discussion of how special education could become nonspecial.
3. Weintraub (2012, p. 53); see also Bateman (2017); Martin (2013).
4. Kauffman (2015d); Gerber (2017).
5. Kauffman and Landrum (2007); Pullen and Hallahan (2015).
6. For further discussion, see Berninger et al. (2002).
7. See Kauffman and Landrum (2018); Kauffman, Pullen, Mostert, and Trent (2011); Kauffman, Nelson, Simpson, and Ward (2017).
8. Rhode, Jenson, and Reavis (2010).
9. Zigmond (1997, p. 389).
10. Zigmond (2003, p. 197).
11. Zigmond and Kloo (2017, p. 259).

chapter 5

Tiers of Education

RTI, MTSS, PBIS. . .

The fact that special can be "sort of" to "very" special—that special education exists on a continuum—has been used in arguing that general and special education can, should, or must be merged. Some education reformers have seized upon it as a way of explaining how *all* students, without exception, can be accommodated in general education with no need for any special classes or schools. In traditional education, for a bit over a century there have been essentially two "tiers" of education: general education (the usual tier for students without identified disabilities) and special education (a second tier for students with special needs calling for special education). And within that second tier there have been what might be called "sub-tiers" of different levels of integration into general education, e.g., general education classroom with supplemental special education (such as consultation), resource room, self-contained classroom, special education day school, special education residential school. This sub-tiered system was the brainchild of Evelyn Deno (1970), who first referred to it as a "Cascade of Services," and that has been referred to at times as the *Continuum of Alternative Placements* (CAPs).[1] For nearly 50 years, special education

> For nearly 50 years, special education regulations, professionals, and federal and state courts have required the Continuum of Alternative Placements (CAPs) as the definitive service delivery model for students with disabilities.

regulations, professionals, and federal and state courts have required CAPs as the definitive service delivery model for students with disabilities.

The Idea of Tiers

The "tiered" structure that has become popular more recently (since the 1990s, but especially since the early twenty-first century) and known primarily as *RTI* (or RtI; I representing *Instruction* or *Intervention*), *MTSS* (multi-tiered systems of supports), and *PBIS* (positive behavioral interventions and supports), proposes adding a *third* tier. We discuss these three frameworks—RTI, MTSS, and PBIS—in this chapter, but we realize that additional frameworks and acronyms for them will likely be invented, hence the "..." in the title of this chapter. In fact, already the list has expanded: another framework related to RTI and its variants is known as CEIS—coordinated early intervening services.[2]

The idea that MTSS, PBIS, and RTI have similar goals and differ more in name than concept is heightened by a letter from the federal Office of Special Education and Rehabilitative Services in 2015:

> For those students who may need additional academic and behavioral supports to succeed in a general education environment, schools may choose to implement a multi-tiered system of supports (MTSS), such as response to intervention (RTI) or positive behavioral interventions and supports (PBIS). MTSS is a schoolwide approach that addresses the needs of all students, including struggling

learners and students with disabilities, and integrates assessment and intervention within a multi-level instructional and behavioral system to maximize student achievement and reduce problem behaviors.[3]

The concept and rhetorical use of the word "framework" is important in all tiered plans. Advocates of tiered plans of education argue that their plan is only a framework for providing services, not services themselves. Thus, they argue, it is inaccurate to speak of a "Tier 1 intervention" or a "Tier 3 student." The tiers simply structure an increasingly focused, individualized education. The three tiers have typically been represented graphically as an isosceles triangle with Tier 1 at the bottom or base and occupying the majority of the triangle's area; Tier 2 is in the middle with a much smaller area; and Tier 3 occupies just a relatively tiny portion of the triangle at its peak.

In all the frameworks we discuss, the assumption is that Tier 1 represents good general education. The great majority of students respond well to such instruction and have no particular learning problems. Approximately 80 percent of students are expected to respond well to Tier 1. Tier 2 is for learners who are struggling in the general education curriculum even with good, evidence-based instruction that is successful with most students. Estimates are that about 15 percent of students will need Tier 2. These students are provided extra resources or a more intensive level of support: for example, they may meet in a small group with a reading specialist for additional instruction or have access to an interactive website that provides extra skills practice. Most frameworks do not consider Tier 2 special education, just additional help or supplemental supports to which the student may respond successfully. But Tier 2 is not exactly general education as usual either; it's meant to be "sort of special," in that it is not typical; nevertheless it is not the same as "special education." If students do not respond adequately to Tier 2 instruction, then they are moved to Tier 3, a more intensive and individualized level of support to which they are expected to respond successfully. For example, these students may receive some one-on-one instruction from a trained paraprofessional or participate in an afterschool tutoring program. About 5 percent of students are expected to need Tier 3. Whether Tier 3 is or is not special education is not clear or consistent across frameworks (in some formulations, the student is *referred* for evaluation for Special Education, i.e., Tier 3), but we have seen no suggestion of a fourth tier nor any discussion of services or placement outside of general education. If tiered instruction is supposed to include all students, we are left to wonder what should be done with students whose response to Tier 3 instruction is not adequate. We could suppose that no students will respond inadequately to Tier 3 instruction, but that supposes that Tier 3 *is* special education in all its forms.

Tiers and Full Inclusion

The assumption of some proponents of educational tiers is that all educational services, special or not, can be included in a tier of general education. Although not every advocate of tiers is a proponent of full inclusion, some use the idea of tiers to promote the practice of serving all students with disabilities in the general education classroom. Strong proponents of full inclusion have constructed a website that includes repetition of the statement "all means all." One of these proponents has written, "I recommend operating schoolwide RTI models without having any separate special education classrooms."[4] In this way, the idea of tiers can be used to eliminate the need for placements other than the general education classroom.

Special Education as Service, Not Place

Some argue that defining special education as a service, not a place, is a *new* concept or a *re*conceptualization of special education. But it is not. Special education has always been a *service* deliverable in a variety of *places*. The fact that special education is actually a service and not a place is used by some to argue that place is irrelevant because, in their view, there is only *one* appropriate and least restrictive placement for all students: the neighborhood public school's general education classroom. They argue that, in order to assure nondiscrimination on any basis, the general education classroom should welcome *all* students and reject *none*, regardless of individual characteristics or educational needs.[5]

In the past, there were instances of special education not being practiced in general education when it could have been. In the late nineteenth and early twentieth centuries, most people thought that delivering special education services *always or nearly always* required a special place, such as a special class or school. Now, we know this not to be true, but the most radical proponents of "full inclusion" argue the opposite of the earlier misunderstanding—that special education services *never or almost never* require a special place. This is an unfortunate misunderstanding, an insistence that something is true when it is not.

Edwin Martin, Jr., the nation's first Assistant Secretary of Education for Special Education and Rehabilitative Services to head the newly created Office of Special Education and Rehabilitative Services (OSERS) who was deeply involved in the crafting and passage of the law we now call IDEA, said this about the history of the notion of a single placement (regardless of whether it is the general education classroom): "My point is that this [IDEA's] history needs to be recalled and 'one choice placements' had failed terribly, without appropriate services, including intensive instruction in a variety of settings."[6] That is, history has taught us that a single placement option has *never* worked to the benefit of *all* individuals with disabilities, thus IDEA specifies the requirement of a *full continuum of alternative placements* (CAP), which includes general education classrooms but also other settings.

> [H]istory has taught us that a single placement option has *never* worked to the benefit of *all* individuals with disabilities, thus IDEA specifies the requirement of a *full continuum of alternative placements* (CAP), which includes general education classrooms but also other settings.

tiers of education: RTI, MTSS, PBIS . . .

Tiers as Prevention of Disabilities

The idea of tiers (above Tier 1) as representing a "sort of" special education is that students with disabilities often start showing signs of difficulty before their difficulties become pronounced. With appropriate early intervention, educators may be able to prevent learning and behavioral *difficulties* from becoming *disabilities*. Thus, it is argued, if all students receive the supports and services they need in general education, and if problems are detected early and "nipped in the bud," many students with special needs won't ever develop "full blown" disabilities and need the typical special education with all its costs, regulations, and requirements.

Early identification of problems and targeted interventions are critical to keep them from worsening. However, we are not convinced that multi-tiered education will be any more effective at preventing disabilities than the current two-tiered system of general and special education.

Avoidance of Special Education Problems

If tiered models of education are intended to be an improvement on the current system, one would assume that many of the problems of the current system would be addressed and solved within the new models. Among special education's most discussed problems are: separation of students from the mainstream (often called "segregation"); sorting, classifying, or labeling individuals; and the social stigma that goes with the afore-mentioned problems.[7] Frameworks of tiers can avoid these problems, so it is argued, because students with disabilities are, in fact, taught in general education classrooms regardless of the

> [W]e are not convinced that multi-tiered education will be any more effective at preventing dis-abilities than the current two-tiered system of general and special education.

nature or severity of their disability. After all, tiered frameworks don't separate students into special places (all students are in a general education classroom); label or "sort" students (only the services are categorized, labeled, or sorted, not students); or stigmatize students (because students aren't separated or labeled). We comment later on these claims.

Inclusion as Celebration of Diversity

Another argument for tiers in education is that students are included in a school community that "celebrates diversity," one in which individual differences of all kinds are considered the norm, not the exception. If students with disabilities are included in such a welcoming community of individuals, then they don't need preparation for inclusion later in life— they will already have experienced it. An assumption is made that by educating all students in the same place regardless of individual needs, both those with and those without disabilities will accept the fact of difference, become accustomed to its accommodation, and learn to value each person's individuality. All students will learn the values of togetherness, mutual respect, and mutual support. At the same time, the quality of instruction will not be diminished in the pursuit of these goals.

A Perspective on Tiered Education

A great temptation is to see things as binary—good/bad, on/off, black/white. But many things in education are nuanced, tiers among them. The idea of tiers is neither all good nor all bad. True, sometimes we need to make overall binary judgments— yes or no—but in many cases that is after we look at both the positive and the negative.

Next, we summarize our thinking about the advantages and disadvantages of tiers—the things we clearly support, the things that raise important questions, and the things that may actually undermine the best instruction for students with disabilities.

Advantages of Tiered Education

The concept of tiered instruction emerged for good reason. The traditional two tiers of education—general and special—present serious problems. Both excluding and including all students with disabilities in public and private education are problematic. Early detection of academic and behavioral problems and effective implementation of evidence-based interventions are complex and often expensive, at least in the short term. Tiered education models may offer some advantages.

Resources for Struggling Learners

Among the advantages of tiers and "sort of" special education is the fact that some students struggle with the standard general education curriculum but do not meet the criteria for having a disability. So, Tier 2 makes it possible to identify and support these students without doing what is considered "full-bore" special education: this is a good idea. Providing resources and interventions for struggling students short of offering the full spectrum of special education services and meeting all the legal requirements of special education makes sense.

Possible Prevention of Problems

Identifying struggling students early makes prevention possible. Intervening to keep small problems from becoming large ones is a good idea. Thus, tiered education offers the possibility of catching problems early and preventing the need for more intensive intervention later. To the extent that general education teachers are aware of "precursors" of later, more serious, and

> Tiered education models may offer some advantages. . . . Providing resources and interventions for struggling students short of offering the full spectrum of special education services . . . makes sense.

more intractable problems, tiers may offer greater hope than traditional special education.

Disadvantages and Possible Problems with Tiers

A major disadvantage of a tiered framework of education is that it solves none of the problems for which special education has been criticized, problems that just seem to "go with the territory" or are intrinsic to any plan or framework for providing appropriate special help for students not doing well in school.[8]

Reasonable Questions about Tiers

Two tiers—the traditional general-special education divide— raise many questions. Three tiers raise many more. The following list of questions is not exhaustive. But one question often leads to the next, and then another, and so on.

- Who decides the tier in which a student is placed to begin with? For example, is it appropriate for some students to go directly to tier 2 or tier 3 (or a higher tier, if there is one)? How much failure is required (or for how long must a student fail) before the instruction offered in any tier is judged unsuccessful? Can a teacher alone decide that a student needs a higher tier than 1? If the decision is made by a team and the classroom teacher disagrees, how is such disagreement handled?
- Who decides that the instruction offered in any tier is sufficiently evidence-based? Are the interventions offered in any given tier identical for all students in that tier? Who implements the various tiers? Should there be a team? Who decides who makes up the team? Are all teachers trained and competent in delivering instruction on all tiers?
- How much progress is enough to conclude that the student has been sufficiently responsive to the instruction offered in a tier? For how long does the student continue to receive instruction (on a tier higher than 1) after being considered "responsive" to it? Does he/she drop to a lower tier (more ordinary, less specialized or less individualized instruction)

after a certain amount of time? What if he/she starts failing again?

- What tier, if any, is considered special education? If no tier is actually special education, then are no students thought to need it? To what tier or tiers do the special education legal requirements and regulations apply? Where in a tiered system does an IEP apply? Are IEPs unrelated to tiers?
- If special education is a separate tier of its own, then who decides, and how, that a student needs it? Must he/she progress (or fail) through all the other tiers before being considered to need special education? Which resources, interventions, or supports are considered special education, and which are not? How are they different from those considered general education?
- If students are taught by a team of teachers and have different peer groups for various activities during the school day, how do they develop close relationships with peers and teachers? How do these factors affect the level of structure and predictability in a student's school day? Do more teachers and more groups mean more transitions and more distractions for students who find them difficult?
- Do the tiers apply to non-academic subjects, like music, art, and physical education? If not, what happens when students need extra supports or interventions in these areas?
- How are money and personnel distributed among the tiers? If all tiers get equal resources, then what are the implications for special education? If the highest tier receives the greatest resources, then how is this a more equitable division of resources than the traditional two-tiered, general and special education framework?
- If resources identified for special education are spent in general education to keep students from needing a higher tier, then what is to prevent special education (or the highest tier) from becoming a true dumping ground—a tier in which students are given comparatively little in the way of supports?
- How many tiers are needed to provide effective resources and interventions for literally *all* students, such that none is excluded or poorly taught? Will some soon suggest there

should there be more than three tiers? Should each student be in a tier of his/her own?

- How will stigma be avoided? Will all tiers higher than the first carry stigma? How will needing extra supports or interventions in the regular classroom not be stigmatizing? Will students (and others) not figure out who the "problem students" are (academically and/or behaviorally)?
- If a student is in the tier considered special education for all academic instruction, must that instruction be delivered in a general education classroom? If so, how will the instruction be delivered effectively without distracting students receiving instruction in other tiers? Will teachers need to have appropriate materials to teach all levels and provide all interventions for all tiers in one classroom?
- If a student is in the tier considered special education for all academic instruction and that instruction is delivered in a separate, dedicated environment, not the general education classroom, then how is the structure different from the traditional two tiers of general and special education for that student?

The Role of Teacher Judgment

Many of the questions above begin with "who" and involve the role of teachers and other individuals in making decisions about a student's needs, progress, failure, response, etc. A persistent problem in all of education, but especially special education, is that someone has to make judgments—draw lines—about lots of things, including which students do or do not need various supports or instruction.

> A persistent problem in all of education, but especially special education, is that someone has to make judgments—draw lines—about lots of things, including which students ... need various supports or instruction.

One difficulty in implementing any level of intervention, whether the traditional two-tiered special/general education or any of the three-tiered frameworks, is the role of teacher judgment in assigning a student to a tier. How much judgment teachers should be allowed to exercise has been a matter of intense debate and sometimes extremes of trust or distrust.

At one extreme was the common practice, before the federal law now known as IDEA was passed in 1975, of a teacher or principal alone deciding that a student should be in special education. All the teacher or principal needed to do was move a cumulative folder and place the student in special education. No need for testing, consultation with parents, or other procedures— just do it. Current law requires a decision by a multidisciplinary committee and communication with parents, including parental agreement to place the child in special education. An individual (usually the teacher) initiates action by making a *referral for evaluation* for special education, but no one can make the placement alone. This seems a reasonable constraint on teacher judgment, but it has resulted in considerable criticism of teacher referrals. Just how tiers are to work in response to teacher judgment needs clarification.

Starting in the late 1970s, psychologists and teacher educators initiated what has become, in our view, extreme distrust of teacher judgment. Some wrote that teacher referral for evaluation was tantamount to placement of students in special education because 80 percent or 90 percent of teacher referrals eventually resulted in the student's being found eligible for and placed in special education.[9] Some critics considered this unacceptable. However, one might wonder what percentage of the time teachers *should* be correct in their judgments? Why shouldn't 80 percent or 90 percent be considered validation of teachers' referrals? And if a student *is* found eligible for special education, wouldn't it follow that he or she would be "placed" or receive special education services? Eventually, although the "scandal" of referral-to-placement might be considered "manufactured," steps were devised to reduce what were considered unnecessary referrals.

The first attempt to reduce referrals, starting in the late 1970s, was called "pre-referral" strategies or interventions. Teachers were advised to try various instructional or behavior management strategies before making a referral. The idea was that teachers often simply had not tried recommended strategies or techniques before concluding that the student needed special education.[10]

Subsequently, in the 1980s, the idea of expected or compulsory pre-referral was ensconced in the first tiered framework, response to intervention (RTI). The basic idea was later included in other tiered frameworks like multi-tiered systems of support (MTSS) and positive behavioral interventions and supports (PBIS). In essence, pre-referral strategies are intended to provide a "paper trail" to document a teacher's efforts to support a struggling student and, if appropriate, back up the claim that the student may have a disability.

Scholar Mike Gerber has noted that teachers' judgment has been and remains the real "test" of how a student is doing and what the student needs.[11] Nevertheless, the role of teacher judgment in any framework, IDEA or MTSS or other tiered framework, continues to be controversial. We do know, at least in broad outlines, the role of teacher judgment under IDEA. We do not know, at this point, the role of teacher judgment in deciding whether a student should receive Tier 1, Tier 2, or Tier 3 instruction in any of the three-tiered frameworks.

Problems Tiers Do Not Solve

Some problems seem inevitable if a special program is to be had, whether special education or anything else (e.g., financial assistance, health care, child protective services). The problems inherent in having a special or different program must not be allowed to eliminate the program (i.e., the perfect must not be allowed to become the enemy of the good). Neither must we allow a proposed "fix" that doesn't really solve a problem to distract us from the problem it purportedly solves.

Anything "special" (i.e., not everyone receives it) faces problems, which critics will predictably use to argue that a new structure or paradigm is needed. Sometimes, a new idea or paradigm *is* needed; but sometimes the "new" is no improvement at all or even makes matters worse. We look at some of the problems for which special education has long been criticized or called a failure. In a few cases, we argue that tiered approaches may actually make the situation *worse* than it is currently; in other cases, we simply name the problem and encourage readers to consider *if* and *how* tiered education will be an improvement.

Variability in Teacher Competence

Our best guess is that tiers done well may be terrific policy and practice, but we also think that relatively few teachers have the sophisticated expertise in assessment and instruction required to make three tiers better than two, much less make full inclusion work well for all students. We conclude this partly because special education has never instilled in all of its *own* teachers, much less general education teachers, the skills needed to make the current system work consistently and as intended.

Training and implementation have fallen short because teaching students with disabilities well is very complex. Logical thinking alone leads to the conclusion that adding "tiers" (beyond the traditional two) inevitably increases complexity and challenges for teachers and teacher educators, particularly if the goal is *full inclusion* (all students taught in one place).

More on Professional Judgment

One of the problems for which special education has been criticized or found wanting is the unavoidable problem that

> Tiers done well may be terrific policy and practice, but ... relatively few teachers have the sophisticated expertise ... to make three tiers better than two. ... [S]pecial education has never instilled in all of its *own* teachers, much less general education teachers, the skills needed to make the current system work [...] [T]eaching students with disabilities well is very complex. ... dding "tiers" ... inevitably increases complexity and challenges ... particularly if the goal is *full inclusion* (all students taught in one place).

someone must use *judgment* (i.e., make decisions about who, what, where, and how within any number of tiers).[12] Adding tiers multiplies these judgments (i.e., as the number of tiers increases, so does the number of decisions that need to be made). This is not difficult to understand. Determining the tier that is most appropriate for a given student requires that students be sorted by what they need to learn or can do. Someone must make decisions about students' tiers, and those decisions will be imperfect, just as they are with two tiers, general and special education. With such decisions—called "sorting," an unavoidable decision process—all the other problems follow.

Labeling and Stigma

Much has been said and written about the "damaging" effects of labeling students in order to talk about their disabilities and the "demoralizing" social stigma attached to being in special education. Although we question the validity of these claims and have written elsewhere on this topic, we do question how multi-tiered systems will avoid labeling and stigma. Sure, one could argue that labeling a level of services is better than labeling an individual student, but common sense and past experience suggest that people will most likely refer to "Tier 3 kids" in much the same way as they refer to "special ed. kids" today. Furthermore, if all supplemental supports and services are to be delivered in the same place (general education classroom), how will the stigmatization of struggling learners, who may be working on skills significantly below grade level, be reduced? We know of students who truly "blossomed" in their special education classroom, where they could be successful academically because the work was instructionally appropriate, and they could feel less isolated socially because they were with other students who understood and shared their struggles. Compassion for others and acceptance of differences are values that can be taught in any setting; we don't have to sacrifice the fundamental characteristics of good specialized instruction (direct, relentless, structured, well-paced, etc.) in a misguided attempt to be "inclusive."

> **C**ompassion for others and acceptance of differences are values that can be taught in any setting; we don't have to sacrifice the fundamental characteristics of good specialized instruction (direct, relentless, structured, well-paced, etc.) in a misguided attempt to be "inclusive."

Other Problems to Consider

As stated previously, if a new paradigm or framework is truly needed, then that new paradigm or framework should purport to "fix" many, if not all, of the problems with whatever it is replacing. Above, we discussed several areas in which we believe a multi-tiered approach may actually be *worse* than the current two-tiered system of general and special education. But many other issues for which special education has long been criticized are simply not addressed by adding tiers, and we can see nothing about multi-tiered systems that would prevent them from falling under the same criticisms. Among these issues are:

- **Arbitrary criteria for identification:** Someone will need to draw lines between students in one tier and students in another. The criteria for drawing these lines may be based on a variety of measures, but the *lines* between a "yes" and a "no" decision will inevitably be arbitrary. Therefore, there will always be individuals who are very close to the line, increasing the probability that errors may occur. Some students will become "false positives" (identified as needing a higher tier when they actually don't); others will be false negatives (determined *not* to need a higher tier when they actually do). This is a persistent problem that tiers will not solve.

- **Ethnic and socioeconomic disproportionality in identification for special services:** Much has been written about the disproportionate representation of ethnic minorities and/or low-income students in special education. Nothing about adding tiers to the system is likely to change the proportions of students from various ethnic/socioeconomic groups who are identified as needing additional help to succeed in school.

- **High cost per student:** Providing specialized instruction and targeted interventions to students who need them costs more than giving everyone the same thing. If multi-tiered approaches will truly identify problems earlier and provide extra supports sooner than the current system, they will require even *more* funding and resources, at least in the short term.

- **Curriculum different from that provided to most students:** Disability, like anything else we measure, occurs on a distribution from "just a little" to "very significantly." Many, if not most, students with disabilities can and should learn much, if not most, of the same things typical students learn. However, there will always be individuals at the extremes of the distribution whose achievement is so significantly behind their peers that they cannot possibly learn the same things. Indeed, these students' learning needs are very, very different from typical students. How will students who need a curriculum other than the general education curriculum be accommodated in a multi-tiered system?

We think the only way to avoid problems like these is to have only a single tier of education, which includes no "special" services for anyone. The claim that any of these problems, and perhaps others as well, can be avoided by adding tiers is a false claim. Sound arguments in favor of more than two tiers may be made. However, arguments that tiers will solve or reduce these problems are not credible.

Furthermore, the relationship between special education and tiers must be clarified. Particularly important will be clarification of which tier(s), if any, are special education and what legal guarantees and regulations in IDEA apply or do not apply to a student in a given tier. Perhaps some will argue that special education permeates all tiers, and a student with an IEP could be in any tier. This begs the question of how special and general education may or may not be different. If special education can be part of instruction in any tier, then tiers would appear to be only general education's structure, not that of special education. One might then wonder whether, in fact, general and special education have been merged into a system of full inclusion. If special education has no identity aside from tiers, then its identity has been absorbed into general education. Whether this is good news or bad is likely a function of how someone sees the special education story.[13]

Summary

Traditional special education is a framework of two tiers: general and special education. Traditional special education has also been governed by the federal law known as IDEA. Several frameworks of three tiers are being tried: RTI (response to instruction), MTSS (multi-tiered systems of supports), and PBIS (positive behavioral interventions and supports). The idea of three tiers is neither all good nor all bad. Three-tiered systems do provide some advantages and make some things more likely or possible, but they do not address special education's core problems, and may even make some problems worse.

Box 5.1 Case in point

Jimmy's teachers know he struggles with reading in particular, so they didn't let him fail and struggle long in the sixth grade. They quickly decided that he needs special help. He has two teachers, and both agree he is not going to meet expectations for sixth grade reading and needs extra help. What they don't really agree on is just how much help he needs. One teacher believes what he is receiving should be classified as Tier 2 resources, the other that he is best served in Tier 3. The specially trained teacher, considered a special education resource teacher, doesn't really care what tier her teaching is considered, just that it is recognized as special education. Jimmy has an IEP that calls for special education in reading. Other students getting the same special instruction Jimmy is receiving do not have IEPs. The school administrators are trying to figure out why some students receive treatment or legal protections that others do not and how tiers are related to special education and to IEPs.

Notes

1. Deno (1970), U.S. Department of Education (2018).
2. See Memorandum (2008).
3. See Letter (2015).
4. The website is SWIFT schools, www.swiftschools.org (2017). The quotation is Sailor (2009, p. 123).
5. E.g., Sailor (2009); Sailor and McCart (2014); SWIFT schools (2017).
6. Martin (2017); See also Imray and Colley (2017).
7. Kauffman, Anastasiou, and Maag (2017).
8. These initial questions were posed by Kauffman, Badar, and Wiley (in press).
9. E.g., Algozzine, Christenson, and Ysseldyke (1982).
10. See Kauffman, Badar, and Wiley (in press); Kauffman, Bruce, and Lloyd (2012).
11. Gerber (2005); Gerber and Semmel (1984).
12. Bateman (1994, 2007; 2017); Bateman, Lloyd, and Tankersley (2015); Kauffman, Anastasiou, and Maag (2017).
13. Kauffman (1999–2000).

chapter 6

Frequent Criticisms and Responses to Them

We recognize the fact that special education is often rightly criticized. Certainly, it has its failures and faults. However, many critics misunderstand what special education is and can do. Special education has been criticized for many reasons. The following are common complaints we hear or read:

1. It is a failure because it does not produce good outcomes.
2. It costs too much.
3. It serves too many students, including many without real disabilities.
4. Its identification procedures are unreliable; there is too much uncertainty about who needs it and who doesn't.
5. It stigmatizes students and ruins their identities, often for life.
6. It serves students for too many years: Once a student gets in, he or she rarely gets back out.
7. It needs to be reconceptualized as a service, not a place.

In this chapter, we first offer our responses to each of these criticisms. Then, we address some frequent questions about special education. We hope that you will be able to answer these questions based on your reading to this point, but we offer our own short answers as a reiteration of our discussion in previous chapters.

Responses to Criticisms

Outcomes Not Good

An important question about every kind of education is what happens to student outcomes when it "works" as it should. If special education works as it should, then what is the result? The results or outcomes are usually measured by performance on standardized tests of academic achievement or on criteria said to measure "success," such as employment, earnings, and independent living without the use of social services or with fewer or less intense social services than predicted.

Critics of special education are prone to comparing outcomes for students with disabilities with those of students *without* disabilities—to presume that if special education really works, then there will be no significant difference between outcomes for students with disabilities and those without disabilities. This kind of comparison is unfair, misleading, and based on denial that many students have disabilities that directly affect academic achievement and social competence.

> Critics of special education often compare outcomes for students with disabilities with those of students *without* disabilities—to presume that if special education really works, then there will be no significant difference between outcomes for students with disabilities and those without disabilities. This kind of comparison is unfair [...] A more reasonable assessment ... is what students with disabilities achieve *with* special education compared with what those with similar disabilities achieve *without* it. That is, does special education help students with disabilities do better than they would otherwise?

A more reasonable assessment of the outcomes of special education is what students with disabilities achieve *with* special education compared with what those with similar disabilities achieve *without* it. That is, does special education help students with disabilities do better than they would otherwise? No one knows precisely how to answer this question for very understandable reasons: difficulty in doing rigorous scientific experiments. Such experiments would require that students considered to need special education be *randomly assigned*: Half to receive special education and the other half not to receive it. This is impossible without a waiver of legal and ethical standards. The law requires that those identified be served; professional ethics demand that students needing help receive it. So, experiments that would address the issue experimentally appear to be impossible. When critics of special education argue that the outcomes are not good, what logic and evidence do they use? Unfortunately, their arguments too often depend on nonsensical comparisons, denying that students with disabilities actually have disabilities that depress their achievement, and on expecting special education to perform true miracles.[1]

What logic and evidence do we use, then, to argue that the outcomes of special education are better than critics portray? Our logic is that the reasonable or valid comparison would be special education for students with disabilities versus no special education for students with similar disabilities. Although experimental data suggesting that special education is better than no special education do not exist (for reasons we have mentioned), there are anecdotes and nonexperimental studies supporting the value of special education to students with disabilities. At least

---

At least one nonexperimental study [Hanushek, Kain, & Rivkin, 2002] involving thousands of students and using sophisticated statistical procedures has found evidence that special education raises the achievement of students with disabilities over what it would have been without special education.

---

one nonexperimental study involving thousands of students and using sophisticated statistical procedures has found evidence that special education raises the achievement of students with disabilities over what it would have been without special education.[2]

Furthermore, we can find many anecdotes to illustrate how the lives of students are typically made better, not worse, by having received special education. Consider the personal story of Leonard E. Wright,

> who arrived [at the Staunton, Virginia, School for the Deaf] as a deaf 8-year-old in 1959, knowing no sign language and unable to communicate even with his parents. By Christmas, he was fluent [in signing]. Wright graduated in 1970, went to college and became a teacher of deaf children.
>
> "The school allowed me the opportunity to be involved fully—literacy clubs, the drama clubs, Boy Scouts," he said through an interpreter [of signing]. "They molded me into what I am."[3]

Or, consider the following story told by a teacher of young children with intellectual disabilities about changes of one of her students and the attitudes of this student's parents toward special education:

> After a few weeks of Alice's placement in my [special self-contained classroom], the parents and I met again. They seemed much happier. "Alice enjoys coming to school now," they let me know. The dad, much to his credit, wished that he had not denied her services in the fall. "She feels so much better about herself now," he said.
>
> Two years later, Alice's father and I talked about his reaction to the eligibility meeting (the one deciding that Alice qualified for my services). "There were so many people," he said, "and they were all saying that there was something terribly wrong with my daughter. I wondered who in the hell they were talking about! My pretty little

girl is so loving and funny. How could they say she was retarded?"

"Does it matter what label they put on her? Isn't she still a pretty, funny, loving little girl?"

"Yeah," he laughed. "Except now she can read!"[4]

Costs Too Much

Special education undeniably costs more than general educa-ion.

However, the long-term costs of not having special education are even higher than the costs of having special education because children with disabilities typically do not learn how to become independent, productive citizens without it.

Special education requires extra teachers, either because a general education class in which students with disabilities are included has two teachers rather than one or because the pupil:teacher ratio is lower in special education than in general education—the teacher has fewer students. Many special education programs rely heavily on classroom aides or para-professionals, which also adds cost. Special education costs are also greater because of special transportation of some students, special curriculum materials, special equipment, specialized treatments or therapies (related services to which students with disabilities receiving special education are entitled), and extra administrators. However, in strictly economic terms, teaching students to become citizens who are as productive and inde-pendent as possible is a relative bargain in cost savings over the long term.[5]

> Special education undeniably costs more than general education. [...] However, in strictly economic terms, teaching students to become citizens who are as productive and independent as possible is a relative bargain in cost savings over the long term.

Serves Too Many Students

When IDEA was passed in 1975 (known then as the Education of All Handicapped Children Act or Public Law 94-142), federal officials estimated that millions of children with disabilities were not receiving special education.[6] Nowadays, a common complaint is that special education has grown too large and too many students have been identified as having disabilities and are found eligible for special education. Indeed, the number of children receiving special education grew from about 3.5 million in 1975 to over 5 million in the early twenty-first century. In recent years, the trajectory has been downward for students identified as having disabilities, particularly in the more "judgmental" categories of learning disabilities and emotional disturbance, and intellectual disability.

Because special education serves so many students and comprises a significant part of education budgets, some people have complained that too many conditions are considered disabilities and that many of the students identified have no "true" disability. So, we must consider what percentage of the school population *should* be identified with various disabilities and how we know the difference between a "true" disability and other conditions (e.g., language or cultural differences, academic underachievement because of poor teaching). After all, one of the justifiable assumptions of the popular three-tiered frameworks is that better teaching, not special education, can be sufficient to address some problems that don't rise to the level of disability.

We have shown in previous chapters that answers to many of the questions anyone can ask about disabilities are arbitrary. They are arbitrary because the underlying variables determining just which students should be identified and how many and for what reasons represent continuous statistical distributions—variables that can vary from a little to a lot, with fine gradations being possible. So, it is a matter of judgment.

In some categories of exceptionality, the problem seems to be one of *too few* individuals being identified, not too many, or for students' problems being judged too often not serious enough to require special education. In fact, some school districts have found ways to artificially cap or lower the number of students served.[7]

Unreliable Identification

Some students have disabilities so significant that nearly everyone recognizes them as "disabilities" immediately or after only a very short time. However, the majority of students who have been identified as having a disability or who are likely to be so identified are less clearly, markedly, or unambiguously disabled. They have problems that are better typified as mild than as severe. They are on the margins of disability or, as some have termed it, have a "judgmental" disability.[8]

The criticism that the identification of disabilities is unreliable has merit only if you ignore the nature of statistical distributions of human characteristics. As you may recall from earlier discussion, most of the human characteristics that have to do with disabilities are continuously distributed (i.e., they can range from a very little to a lot, with fine gradations possible). For any such distribution, the line we draw for classification is arbitrary—i.e., can be changed). Moreover, the closer we draw the line to the average, the more cases of uncertainty we will have. We will have more individuals who are close to the criterion (i.e., who are "borderline").[9] Thus, it is to be expected that identification of students with milder disabilities will be less reliable than identification of those with more severe disabilities—who are way out at the extremes of the distribution. Disability is *always* judgmental to some degree.

Besides, it is important to recognize that uncertainty in identification is not unique to the area of disability or to the field of special education. In any area of human functioning, including medicine, differences of opinion are likely to occur when the condition is "borderline." Some cases (e.g., of cancer or of learning disability) are very clear; others are not. Second and third opinions are often sought under such circumstances, and experienced and competent professionals (whether physicians, psychologists, teachers, plumbers, engineers ... whatever the profession or line of work) may disagree.

Stigmatizes Students and Ruins Identity

Stigma and positive self-esteem are both important and difficult issues in special education and other kinds of social service. We want to shelter people from social stigma whenever possible (i.e., to protect them from social rejection and unfair discrimination because of their personal characteristics). We also want to help them develop healthy self-regard, to see themselves as valuable and capable people who share most of the characteristics of those who are not exceptional. This is particularly difficult when the exceptionality is not giftedness but incompetence or inability to perform like most people in a particular part of life.

We clarify here our concern about the possibility of pathological *over* estimation of one's abilities or persistent claims of superiority that are inconsistent with reality. Developing a healthy self-esteem often means increasing it, but sometimes emotional disturbance includes an inflated self-image inconsistent with reality. Inflated self-regard can also be a disability in need of correction.

Understanding that the differences we call disabilities vary markedly and that these differences differ in their significance for certain social roles is critically important. Some differences are trivial, and other differences are tremendously important in education or for other activities. In all societies, an important issue is the best way to eliminate inappropriate stigma and improve realistic self-esteem. However, we need to consider the possible consequences of eliminating all stigma from all exceptionalities in any society.[10]

Perhaps we should recognize that stigma is a reality in any society and that the skillful and humane management of stigma, not its total elimination, is what we should shoot for. In his landmark study of people with intellectual disability, anthropologist Robert Edgerton commented on the universality of stigma (and his use of the word incompetence should be interpreted to mean incompetence to do certain things, not incompetence in general):

> Both incompetence and stigma management are ubiquitous features of any society, for societies cannot fail to be

concerned with the incompetence of their members. Neither can they fail to inflict stigma upon certain, if not all, of their incompetents. Hence, some people in all societies must be both incompetent and stigmatized.[11]

If stigma is ubiquitous or always present in some form in any society, the question becomes how we can best manage or respond to it. Denial that a difference exists (or the pretense that it does not) may allow people to "pass" or to be seen as unexceptional. The gifted person may "pass" as unexceptional in many or most circumstances in which the gift or talent is not featured. The person who cannot perform as expected, and is therefore incompetent at a particular understanding or ability, may be helped to "pass" in many situations. However, what Edgerton described as the "cloak of competence" has substantial limitations in covering up or protecting exceptionality. Edgerton described the cloak and the limits of pretense:

> The [formerly institutionalized people with intellectual disabilities] strive to cover themselves with a protective cloak of competence. To their own satisfaction they manage to locate such coverings, but the cloaks that they think protect them are in reality such tattered and transparent garments that they reveal their wearers in all their naked incompetence. In a sense, these retarded persons are like the emperor in the fairy tale who thought he was wearing the most elegant garments but, in fact, was wearing nothing at all.[12]

Providing "cover" and helping someone "pass" may well be necessary or the most humane thing to do in some circumstances, but such pretense does not address the more fundamental issue of stigma. Empathy, support, accommodation, and acceptance are much more likely to be generated by candid portrayal of a problem, disability, or incompetence. Euphemisms and other dodges of realities are not likely to reduce stigma in the long run.

Writer Martha Randolph Carr described her son Louie's learning disability and her inability to recognize it. She was afraid of labeling her son. Because of her fear, she decided to read to Louie throughout his elementary school years, because he could not read for himself. Louie's response to his disability finally being labeled when he was in high school was very different from what his mother had anticipated. Instead of being hurt or humiliated by the label, he was relieved. He realized he wasn't stupid, and he wondered whether his mother was also worried. Ms. Carr realized that her unwillingness to recognize the truth about Louie was the problem, not labeling.[13]

Special education has struggled with changing words in the hope that a change of words will change social attitudes toward disabilities of various kinds. For example, "mental retardation" is now called "intellectual disability" to try to avoid stigma and increase acceptance. The "R word" is seen as stigmatizing. The American Association on Mental Retardation (AAMR) renamed itself the American Association on Intellectual and Developmental Disorders (AAIDD) to try to reduce the stigma of what was called mental retardation, and the ARC, once the Association for Retarded Citizens, has become simply the "ark". Various disorders and disabilities are now referred to euphemistically as "challenges," which actually fools no one.

Societal attitudes can change, although such change is often relatively slow and difficult. It changes because of understanding, not the words used to describe the problem. Consider how social attitudes toward smoking, drunk driving, homosexuality, and cancer have changed over the past several decades. Smoking was once tolerated nearly everywhere, but that is no longer true. Calling it something other than smoking was not what changed attitudes. Drunk driving, once tolerated or accepted as a given, is now more unacceptable, but not because the words used to describe it were changed. Homosexuality has emerged from the days of cover-up and shame, being described euphemistically

> **V**arious disorders and disabilities are now referred to euphemistically as "challenges," which actually fools no one.

as "the love that dare not speak its name." Attitudes toward homosexuality did not change because of euphemisms. Cancer was once a disease to be hidden by those who had it and by their loved ones and was discussed, if at all, in hushed tones. Now cancer is spoken of openly and dealt with as a serious but increasingly treatable and sometimes preventable disease, but not because it was described with euphemisms.

Perhaps cancer is among the best models for managing the stigma of disability. No mentally healthy individual wants to have cancer, and no mentally healthy person wants to have a disability. Neither is a good thing to have. The stigma of cancer has abated because people were encouraged to confront it for what it is. Cancer is something to be acknowledged and treated. In short, we want people to recognize it for what it is and treat it to minimize its effects. We want people without cancer to take action to prevent it, or at least to reduce the chances of having it. We want our society to be accepting and supportive of those who have cancer even though we realize it is a terrible thing to have. We could do no better than to work for a similar societal response to disability.

The issue of disability carrying stigma was brought home to author Hallahan recently. He was watching an interview on television of a young mother of a child with Down syndrome. She recounted how she had been terribly offended when, after

Cancer was once a disease to be hidden by those who had it and by their loved ones and was discussed, if at all, in hushed tones. Now cancer is spoken of openly and dealt with as a serious but increasingly treatable and sometimes preventable disease, but not because it was described with euphemisms. [. . .] Perhaps cancer is among the best models for managing the stigma of disability. . . . Cancer is something to be acknowledged and treated. . . . We want our society to be accepting and supportive of those who have cancer even though we realize it is a terrible thing to have. We could do no better than to work for a similar societal response to disability.

frequent criticisms and responses to them   123

> he assumption that special education ... *creates* stigma ... confuses the treatment with the cause. Would we make the assumption that the diagnosis and treatment of cancer *caused* the stigma it once carried? Of course not!

telling someone that she had a child with Down syndrome, that the person had said, "I'm sorry." If she had said her child had cancer, would this mother have been offended by the same response from the other person? One could, of course, infer that the person saying he was sorry was thinking that the child was somehow less human because she had Down syndrome. And perhaps because of other interactions the mother had had with people she was quick to infer that that was his intent. But a more literal inference would be that he was sorry because of all the likely hurdles—physical, psychological, and educational—the mother and child would have to face.

In the end, the assumption that special education itself, or identification as needing it, *creates* stigma is pernicious. It confuses the treatment with the cause. Would we make the assumption that the diagnosis and treatment of cancer *caused* the stigma it once carried? Of course not!

Serves Students Too Long

Most of the students who receive special education have *developmental* disabilities of some kind. This means that their conditions are usually permanent, not temporary (although they may get better or worse at times) and there is no known "cure." So, the problem is finding the best way to manage the disability, not necessarily to make it disappear.

Some commentaries reveal a naive view of both special education and the disabilities it addresses. They portray disability as being more like a broken bone or common cold that is a temporary condition, not chronic. And they see special education as designed to be more like a cast or antihistamine than like insulin, which some diabetics will need indefinitely. The conclusion that special education is wasted time and effort because so few students "escape" from it is misguided.

The truth is that most students with disabilities will need special teaching, accommodations, or supports throughout their school experience no matter how efficient or effective special education is. And many if not most will require life-long support or special attention if they are to accomplish all they can. The law requires educators and parents to agree that a student no longer needs special education if he or she is to exit special education (i.e., to be "decertified"). The fact that a small percentage of students are decertified from special education is to be expected, given the nature of developmental disabilities. The irony is that those who are critical of how long students stay in special education—who say that too few students exit special education or are decertified—are often the same people who contend that too many students are being misidentified as needing special education. The irony is that the more obvious the need for special education, the fewer the students who can *ever* be expected to no longer need special education.

Should Be Re-conceptualized as a Service, Not a Place

This is one of the most curious criticisms of special education because, to our knowledge, special education has *always*—since its inception—been conceptualized as a service, not a place. True, people who thought up special education thought the service could best be delivered only in a special classroom or school, but it was the service, not the place itself, that defined special education. We don't know any special education scholar or leader who has written or conceptualized special education merely as a physical or geographical place, not as a service. So, the criticism seems to us to be of the variety many have called a "straw man" or a completely trumped up argument.

Undoubtedly, special education has sometimes been misrepresented as a place, in some cases by the very people who suggest that it be re-conceptualized as a service (e.g., they may argue that the best special education services can be delivered only in a regular classroom, merely the opposite extreme of arguing that it can be delivered only in a special class or school). Sometimes, students have not received or do not receive the special education they deserve, but this absence of the services they deserve is no more peculiar to place than to its delivery. The absence of appropriate special services can mean simply that special education was poorly implemented. Sometimes this is because of the place it is implemented, although that is not always so.

The people who invented special education recognized that special education sometimes requires a special place, simply because no teacher is capable of offering all kinds of instruction in the same place and at the same time. Some students need to be taught things that others don't need. So, as has been recognized all along, the specialized places in which special education sometimes occurs are necessary for some special instruction, especially if that instruction is to be really good.

There is no magic in any place, either the general education classroom or a special class. Place, by itself, doesn't represent good special education.

Special education is neither good nor bad because of *where* it is offered, although the place it is practiced can make it more likely to be better or less likely to be done well. The quality of instruction is what matters most and what makes special education special. But, as we have suggested in previous chapters, if instruction is actually special, then not everyone gets it. And if it is truly special, then not every teacher can provide it in every context. Sometimes, special education demands a special place, but the place does not represent the concept; it does not now, and it never has.

Special education is neither good nor bad because of *where* it is offered, although the place it is practiced can make it more likely to be better or less likely to be done well. The quality of instruction is what matters most and what makes special education special.

Other Questions about Special Education

Following are some of the additional questions reasonable people might ask about special education. We have attempted to answer these questions previously, but here we reiterate our answers in condensed form.

Who Needs Special Education?

The short answer is that special education is intended to serve those students whose school performance is exceptionally high or low because they have special gifts or talents (in the case of exceptionally high performance) or disabilities (in the case of exceptionally low performance) or both. Another way of putting this is that special education is designed to serve students at the fringes or extremes of statistical distributions of performance. Special education is mandated by federal law (IDEA) for students with disabilities, but there is no federal law requiring special education for students with special gifts or talents. Some students are "twice exceptional," meaning they have both disabilities and special gifts or talents. Unfortunately, for those with special gifs or talents, special education is legally required only if they also have disabilities (see Chapter 3).

Who Should Decide Whether a Student Needs Special Education?

This is actually one of special education's perpetual questions— one that isn't going to be answered to everyone's satisfaction because it is a matter of judgment and social convention. The federal law, IDEA, demands that no single individual be allowed to make the decision. The decision is to be made jointly by educators and parents—the people who know the child best and work with him or her the most (see Chapters 2 and 4).

Why Do Some Exceptional Students Not Need Special Education?

Some students have disabilities that do not interfere with their school performance—academic achievement or social adjustment.

That is, some students with disabilities do not need special education simply because their educational performance and social interaction are unaffected. Usually, these are a subgroup of students with physical or sensory disabilities (see Chapter 3).

Why Can't We Know Exactly Who Does and Doesn't Need Special Education?

We do know, in some cases, but we don't know in all cases. In many cases, it's a tough call. People may have serious differences of opinion, but eventually the line must be drawn. The cases close to the line or smack dab on the line are difficult to call. This is simply because abilities (and, therefore, disabilities, too) are related to human characteristics with continuous statistical distributions. The point at which we call something a disability or a gift is arbitrary, and the closer to the typical we draw our line the more cases of uncertainty we encounter. This is true not just for special education but for nearly everything about human beings.

What Kinds of Exceptionalities Require Special Education?

For the most part, the exceptionalities requiring special education include differences in thinking or cognition (either intellectual disabilities or intellect in the gifted range), learning, focusing and sustaining attention, controlling emotions and behavior, communicating, hearing, seeing, physical activity and health, or some combination of these. Some students have both special gifts or talents and disabilities for which special education is needed (see Chapter 3).

The point at which we call something a disability or a gift is arbitrary, and the closer to the typical we draw our line the more cases of uncertainty we encounter. This is true not just for special education but for nearly everything about human beings.

Why Shouldn't All *Students Have Special Education?*

Simply put, it is neither reasonable nor feasible to provide special education for every student. Special implies something atypical, unusual, and different from the norm. First of all, by definition, not all education can be special. Second, the extraordinary effort demanded for special education is not reasonable to expect for all students or all teachers. The education of all students can be and should be good, but it cannot be special for all students (see Chapters 2 and 4).

Why Do We Need Categories and Labels?

Communication is impossible without categories and labels. We need categories and labels to make sense of the world and communicate clearly with other people. True, categories and labels can be wrong and can be used with malice. It's important not to misinterpret a given label, whatever it may be (e.g., tall, obese, deaf, stutterer, cerebral palsy). We must be on our guard against assuming that a label tells us something it does not or reveals everything we need to know about an individual. But without categories and labels we can't describe people or phenomena. Furthermore, the more specifically and reliably we can label something the better we can communicate about it. Vague and general labels result in vague and general communication. The problem of stigma is real and important, but stigma

---

Communication is impossible without categories and labels. . . . True, categories and labels can be wrong and can be used with malice. . . . We must be on our guard against assuming that a label tells us something it does not or reveals everything we need to know about an individual. But without categories and labels we can't describe people or phenomena. . . . The problem of stigma is real and important, but stigma is created by social responses to labels or categories, not the labels or categories themselves.

---

is created by social responses to labels or categories, not the labels or categories themselves (see Chapter 3). Besides, "We must think very carefully about stopping using words simply because they have been mistreated in the past. . . . Not putting a label on it [a disability] does not make it go away."[14]

Why Don't We Call Special Education Something Else?

We could, and perhaps we will someday. We do not think a change in terminology is needed or would improve the education of students with or without disabilities. Changing the label for education designed for exceptional students would not change its nature or substance. Something like "precision teaching" or designation of a tier of education may eventually replace the term "special education," but all the elements of special education would—or, we think, at least should—remain the same (see Chapters 2, 4, and 5).

What Is Special about Special Education?

Special and general education are similar in many respects, often including what is taught and basic instructional procedures. However, compared with general education, special education is more explicit, systematic, intensive, relentless, appropriately paced, and individualized. It also differs in size of instructional group and curriculum, includes more corrective feedback, is characterized by longer and more frequent instruction in areas of particular need, is more highly structured, and includes more positive reinforcement and closer monitoring and assessment.[15]

Why Does Good Education Make Kids Less Alike Rather than More Alike?

Good education is aimed at helping students become even better at what they do well, not just helping those below a standard reach it. Hence, good education increases the variance and range of the statistical distribution of outcomes. Students learn at different rates, and those who are exceptionally fast inevitably become less like those who are slower in acquiring knowledge and ability in particular areas (see Chapter 2). The late physicist Richard Feynman (1985) said, "For instance, in education you increase differences. If someone's good at something, you try to develop his ability, which results in differences, or inequalities."[16]

What Is Wrong with Heterogeneous Grouping for Instruction?

Heterogeneous grouping—grouping together students who differ greatly in knowledge of what is being taught—is boring for those who have already mastered the content and humiliating for those who can't perform adequately. So, it is unsatisfying for students who are very discrepant from the majority of the group in what they know and are able to do. For the teacher, whether a general or special educator, extremely heterogeneous grouping for instruction presents insurmountable difficulty—the necessity of extreme differentiation that very few teachers can handle well. Heterogeneous grouping may be fine for some non-instructional activities, but it is good for neither students nor their teachers when the focus is on instruction (see Chapters 2 and 4).

What Is Wrong with Homogeneous Grouping for Instruction?

Nothing. Some people have suggested that it is unfair because students are "tracked" or because the lower-performing students get the least competent teachers. However, "tracking" refers to rigid assignment to groups, not the flexible homogeneous grouping for instruction that we recommend. And homogeneous grouping for *instruction* does *not* mean that students are homogeneously grouped for *everything* in school (see Chapters 2 and 4).[17]

Why Not Just Treat Every Child as an Individual So that Grouping Is Unnecessary?

There are simply not enough resources, and probably there never will be, to have individualized educational planning and teaching for *all* students. Education, like clothes and cars and many other consumer goods, must be designed for the typical if the masses are to receive it. Individualized education for every student is infeasible for the same reasons that tailor-made clothing (as opposed to clothing bought off the rack) for everyone is infeasible. Perhaps technology will some day allow people to have clothing tailored to them personally. That doesn't necessarily mean the end of typical sizes. The cost of truly personalized education for everyone would likely be prohibitive, even with advanced technology (see Chapter 4).

How Would We Know that Special Education Is Effective?

First, we describe some things that do *not* describe the effectiveness of special education. *More* special education—an increase in the number or percentage of individuals does *not* make it more effective. Increases in money spent on it—its *cost* does *not* mean it's more effective. *Special education is effective if and only if students learn more with it than without it.* However, doing sound scientific experiments to show that it is effective is very difficult because it's not legally and ethically defensible to withhold special education from students who need it—to establish a "control group" through random assignment. So, the best we can do is look at how students with disabilities or special gifts fare before they get special education compared with how they fare after they do. Special education can't be expected to make exceptional students perform like those who are not, but it can improve the quality of life and academic performance of students over what they would have done had they not received special education. Special education is effective to the extent that it provides better instruction than students would have received in general education. Instruction should be the focus, not something else.[18]

Why Can't Every Student Be Average or Better at Something?

The reason is simply that an average is based on a statistical distribution, which always has a part below average. Having

frequent criticisms and responses to them

everyone or everything above average on any given criterion is a mathematical impossibility. There is also a distribution of how many different things a given person is good at. Some are good at many things, some at an average number of things, and some are above average in nothing. Besides, "average" is by definition a moving target (see Chapter 2 and our two previous answers).

Where Do Benchmarks or Criteria for Exit, Promotion, or a Diploma Come From?

Benchmarks or other criteria are based on our expectations of what the typical or average student can achieve. The benchmark may be somewhat higher or lower than the current average, but, ultimately, the average (or typical or normal) is what we expect of students or of ourselves. True, the benchmark for being admitted to a given program (e.g., a military academy, gifted program college, "elite" status, etc.) may be substantially higher than the average. However, the average is always an important reference point in setting a criterion for achievement or non-achievement (see Chapter 2).

Why Is It Impossible for All Students to Reach a Common Standard?

Measurement of anything (academic achievement included) always produces a statistical distribution of scores, and there is always a "behind" or lower segment of the distribution. Those in the lower range of the distribution can be taught well, but good teaching never has and never will eliminate the lower part of the distribution. Only in an imaginary place, like Garrison Keillor's fabled "Lake Wobegon" (where, as he always said on his radio show, *Prairie Home Companion*, "all the children are above average") can all of the children be above average or any other percentile, except the first. Actually, mathematics just dictates that unless the standard is zero, someone will be below it.

We think it's important to recognize this: "Denial of a fact does not alter the fact . . . not liking mathematical truths—there

> Only in an imaginary place, like Garrison Keillor's fabled "Lake Wobegon" (where, as he always said on his radio show, *Prairie Home Companion*, "all the children are above average.... [M]athematics just dictates that unless the standard is zero, someone will be below it.

is a norm and there is a bell curve which indicates the broad parameters of that norm—does not alter the mathematical fact of the norm."[19]

What is the Least Restrictive Environment for a Student?

The least restrictive environment (LRE) for a given student is the environment closest to the one the student would be in if he or she had no disability but—and here's the "kicker"—*given that the instructional needs of the student can be met as specified in the IEP* (individual education program). Federal special education law (IDEA) requires, first, a free appropriate public education (FAPE). By law and rational analysis, FAPE comes first. LRE cannot be decided before FAPE. *After* an appropriate education has been designed for a student (as specified in the IEP), *then and only then* can the LRE be determined. For some students, this will be the general education classroom. For others, it will be a more specialized environment, including, for some, a special class or special school (see Chapters 1 and 4).[20]

What Is Inclusion, and Why Is It a Good Idea Sometimes but Not Always?

Inclusion has been defined in various ways, but it generally refers to educating exceptional students in neighborhood schools and regular classes—the same classrooms as typical students, the classrooms they would attend were they not exceptional. Inclusion is called for as one possibility in IDEA. But federal

frequent criticisms and responses to them

T he LRE includes not only the general education classroom but resource rooms, special self-contained classes, special schools, and teaching in the home or hospital. . . . The law calls for a case-by-case determination of the LRE, not a blanket policy of placement in general education or any other environment. For some students, inclusion in general education is harmful and counter-productive, as the student needs a more specialized and separate educational setting.

law requires inclusion only to the extent appropriate—consistent with the best interests of the student. *Full* inclusion generally refers to placing *all* exceptional children in typical schools and classes regardless of their exceptionality. Full inclusion (meaning no exceptions) is illegal under IDEA, and it is also an unworkable idea. IDEA calls for a full *continuum of alternative placements* (CAP) and requires placement in the *least restrictive environment* (LRE), which should not be interpreted to mean the same environment for all students.

The LRE includes not only the general education classroom but resource rooms, special self-contained classes, special schools, and teaching in the home or hospital, as may be most appropriate for the individual student. The law calls for a case-by-case determination of the LRE, not a blanket policy of placement in general education or any other environment. For some students, inclusion in general education is harmful and counterproductive, as the student needs a more specialized and separate educational setting.[21]

Why Is the Full Inclusion of All Students neither Feasible nor Desirable?

The inclusion of all students in general education is neither feasible nor desirable for several reasons. First, some students need highly specialized, intensive instruction that most students don't (e.g., in use of Braille or orientation and mobility skills, manual communication, specific academic or social skills, self-care). Second, not all teachers of general education have the knowledge and skills required to teach all students what they need to know, and special teachers can't provide the most effective instruction exceptional students need in the context of the general education classroom. Third, typical students deserve the opportunity for effective instruction without the distraction that inevitably results from instructing exceptional students at the same time in the same place. Fourth, it short-circuits the development of a helpful disability culture: Most of us need affiliation with others who share our characteristics of religious beliefs, interests, particular life experiences, abilities, disabilities, and so on. Students with disabilities are no exception in this regard. They often find understanding, support, and increased power in congregation. A blanket policy of full inclusion of all students neglects individual differences that are important for academic and social learning. As one advocate of reasonable inclusion put it, "By blindly pursuing absolute adherence to a concept, [extreme or full] inclusionists have neglected the educational and social needs of individual children."[22] Finally, it's illegal under federal law (IDEA).

Is Special Education a Legitimate Profession?

Some critics have described special education in very derogatory terms, as wasteful, biased, segregating, ineffective, invalid, and so on such that the profession seems to be at a crossroad of identity.[23] However, one of our distinguished colleagues, Hill Walker, made the following comments in accepting an award in 2003 from a professional organization in special education:

> I believe our field stands as a lighthouse beacon of hope, caring and unconditional support for these at-risk children and youth to whom life has dealt such a cruel hand. I have been a researcher in the area of school-related behavior disorders for over three decades. During that time, I have been proud to call myself a member of the field [of emotional and

behavioral disorders] which brings together dedicated professionals from diverse background who work together so well on behalf of at-risk children. Our field models demonstrate positive values and best practices that can make a real difference in the lives of children and youth with emotional and behavioral disorders and those of their families.[24]

Much the same could be said about other areas of special education, which stand for the effort to give all students a fair chance to learn academics and good social behavior. In our opinion, special education is both legitimate and essential to achieving social justice in schooling. Like our colleague Walker, we are proud to be associated with the profession of special education, and we believe special educators in every category of exceptionality are doing essential work. Our hope is not merely that special education survives as a profession but that it becomes everything it should be for every exceptional learner.

What Accounts for the Disproportional Representation of Certain Ethnic Groups and Males in Special Education?

We do not know for certain. The reasons are probably multiple and complex, the same as are the answers to the question about why some students are exceptional. African-American students tend to be over-represented in some categories of special education when raw percentages (of those in the general population and those in special education) are compared. Unfair discrimination or racism and sexism no doubt account for some cases. But we can't ignore the roles of poverty, home experiences, community expectations, genetics, health care, and every other factor known to contribute to the answer to the question of why students have disabilities or special gifts and talents. The more important question for us is whether students who need special education are getting it, regardless of the proportion of any given subpopulation that may be receiving special education (see Chapter 3).[25]

Why Can't Special Education Make Itself Unnecessary through Effective Prevention and Training?

The fact is that not all cases of disability can be prevented. Even with our best instructional, health, and safety procedures, some individuals will have disabilities and need special education. Moreover, although some special education practices can be incorporated into general education, not all of them can be. Nor is being in a regular classroom alongside non-exceptional age peers the best place for all students, regardless of their characteristics and needs.[26] Consequently special education will always be needed, just as emergency medical care and intensive care units and other specialized services will always be needed (e.g., fire departments, hospitals, legal counsel . . .) (see Chapters 2 and 3).

What Disabilities Can Be Prevented?

Many disabilities are preventable by better prenatal care, health care after birth, and safety precautions. Many disabilities can be prevented from becoming worse if we identify them early and provide effective treatment. However, some disabilities are going to occur even with our best efforts to prevent them from occurring at all, and sometimes disabilities are progressive in spite of early identification and the best treatment possible. Human variations and accidents are givens, and we need to be ready to treat and accommodate disabilities regardless of our best preventive efforts (see Chapter 3).

What Do We Know about Prevention?

All of the information we could provide about prevention can't be given in a brief answer. We know that effective *primary* prevention (meaning the problem never surfaces) of learning and behavior problems requires excellent instruction and behavior management for all students, not just exceptional students. Health care and safety procedures can prevent many disabilities related to diseases, accidents, or physiological problems. Effective *secondary* prevention requires early identification of those students who are beginning to have problems (e.g., in learning, behavior, or physical abilities), and special teaching or other intervention to address problems asap. Effective *secondary* prevention either keeps the problem from getting worse or reverses it. *Tertiary* prevention is for cases in which problems are already severe, with the goal of avoiding further complications and limiting the negative effects. In all cases and at all levels, good prevention depends on using procedures known to facilitate normal development and minimize problems (see Chapter 3).[27]

Why Can't We Just Leave Special Education up to Localities and States and Eliminate Federal Laws and Regulations?

That is certainly possible, but we would then be at considerable risk of losing special education in some localities and states. The federal special education law (IDEA) was passed in response to the failure of localities and states to meet the needs of students with disabilities. Special education requires balancing the cost of intrusion of federal education policy against the benefit of a uniform policy of meeting the needs of students with disabilities. We feel that the benefits of federal requirements clearly outweigh their cost.[28]

Why can't we just leave special education up to local and state education agencies and eliminate federal laws and regulations? [. . .] but we would then be at considerable risk of losing special education in some localities and states. The federal special education law (IDEA) was passed in response to the failure of localities and states to meet the needs of students with disabilities. Special education requires balancing the cost of intrusion of federal education policy against the benefit of a uniform policy of meeting the needs of students with disabilities. . . . [T]he benefits of federal requirements clearly outweigh their cost.

Summary

Special education is often criticized as follows: It is a failure because it does not produce good outcomes, costs too much, serves too many students (including many who do not actually have disabilities), is unreliable and unfairly discriminatory in identifying students, creates social stigma and ruins students' identities, keeps students too long and decertifies too few of them, and needs reconceptualization. None of these criticisms is valid, in our opinion. Answering basic questions about special education requires understanding of teaching, students' characteristics, and the realities and meanings of statistical distributions.

Box 6.1 Case in point

- **Were the Outcomes Good in Jimmy's Case?** After a year of special reading instruction, which consisted of 2 hours per day being instructed in a group of 3, and his highly skilled and experienced teacher's use of an evidence-based program, Jimmy has increased his reading level from third grade to fifth grade, although he is still not up to the grade level; he should be on grade 7. We realize that this is not typical and that this was an unusually good delivery of special education services. In too many cases, the teacher has neither the training nor the experience necessary, the group is too large or heterogeneous in instructional needs, the special instruction is not offered with sufficient time and intensity, and the evidence supporting the instructional program is often lacking.

  Jimmy increased his reading level at twice the expected rate (i.e., 2 years' gain in 1 year of schooling), but he is still behind his age mates. We think that is very good progress, although it still leaves Jimmy behind most seventh graders in reading. But he is not as far behind as he would have been without special education. We think he is very, very likely better off than he would be had he not had special education,

So, is the outcome a good one for him? We think so, but it depends on how you look at it.

- **Did Jimmy's Special Education Cost Too Much?** It is difficult to calculate very precisely the cost of Jimmy's special education for the past year. The cost of public education and special education varies considerably from one district to another. Jimmy's special education obviously cost more than if he hadn't had it. But, was the additional cost too high? We don't think so, but anyone can say they think the cost of education is too high, pretty much regardless of what it is. Jimmy will likely be much more employable when he finishes school because he had help in reading, and this is particularly likely if his special education continues.

- **Did Jimmy Unnecessarily Swell the Ranks of Students Getting Special Education?** That depends on whether you think he needed special education. Was it necessary for him to get it? We think so, but others might argue that he could have "caught up" without special education if he'd worked harder and his general education teacher worked harder to make his reading instruction appropriate. Would it have been better to identify his reading problem sooner and give him special instruction? Probably so, in our opinion, although the fact that earlier intervention wasn't provided isn't a logical argument that it should not have been provided later. Earlier may well have been better, but better late than never.

- **Were the Procedures Used to Identify Jimmy so Unreliable that We Still Don't Really Know Whether He Needed Special Education?** The tests given to Jimmy were not perfect, and they have margins of error. However, it doesn't look to us as if they were grossly inaccurate in assessing Jimmy's performance or in determining appropriate expectations for his learning.

- **Was Jimmy Unnecessarily Stigmatized or Was His Identity Ruined by Receiving Special Education?** Some of Jimmy's classmates teased him about his going to a special education room. Most did not. Jimmy's teacher called him aside and asked him privately whether she could talk to those who teased him. With his permission, she had private conversations with the students who teased, letting them know she was aware of it, wanted it to stop, and explaining that some students need extra help on some things and that was no excuse to tease them. Jimmy was sorry to be identified as failing to meet expectations and receive special education, but he is very happy with his progress. We know that having any problem, regardless of its nature, carries a certain amount of stigma. But we don't see his identity as having been ruined. Nor do we see the possible stigma as being worse than the frustration, low self-esteem, and anxiety he might have faced had he been left to fail more and fall further behind his classmates in reading skill.

- **Did Jimmy's Special Education "Fail" because He Still Required those Services after a Year?** Jimmy has received special education for one year and has still not reached his grade level in reading. Therefore, his parents and teachers want his special education to continue. He and his parents know that he has a learning disability. Their understanding is that he's likely to struggle throughout his life with his learning disability. They are not so concerned about his "getting out" of special education as they are about his receiving the special instruction he needs now and for as long as he needs it.

- **Can the Special Education Jimmy Received Be Best Conceptualized as a Place or as a Service?** Jimmy received special instruction. That is a service. It was not feasible for his general education teacher to give him the specialized instruction and extra attention his learning disability required. His special education was not a matter of getting him to a certain location but giving him the instruction he needed. The place he went for that instruction was important only because it allowed the service to be provided most effectively and efficiently.

frequent criticisms and responses to them

Notes

1. Kauffman (2005, 2008).
2. Hanushek, Kain, and Rivkin (2002).
3. Helderman (2003, p, B7).
4. Kauffman and Pullen (1996, p. 8). See also Carpenter and Bovair (1996), Kauffman, Bantz, and McCullough (2002).
5. E.g., see Lynch (2004).
6. Kauffman (1983).
7. See Forness et al. (2012); Kauffman and Badar (2018); Rosenthal (2016); Rosenthal and Barned-Smith (2016).
8. See Kauffman and Lloyd (2017).
9. Kauffman and Lloyd (2017).
10. Kauffman and Badar (2013, 2017, 2018).
11. Edgerton (1967, p. 218).
12. Edgerton (1993, p. 193).
13. Carr (2004).
14. Imray and Colley (2017). For further discussion of labels and categories, see Kauffman and Badar (2014a).
15. For book-length treatment of what makes special education special, see Cook and Shirmer (2006).
16. Feynman (1985, p. 281); see also Kauffman (2015b); Kauffman and Lloyd (2017); For discussion of why science is important in special education, see Kauffman (2011), Landrum (2015), and Sasso (2001).
17. For more on homogeneous and heterogeneous grouping for instruction, see Kauffman (2011).
18. The importance of a focus on instruction rather than place is further clarified by Bateman (2004); Imray and Colley (2017); Kauffman and Badar (2014b, 2016); Pullen and Hallahan (2015).
19. Imray and Colley (2017, p. 53).
20. For more discussion of FAPE and its relationship to LRE, see Yell (2015) and Yell, Katsiyannis, and Bradley (2017).
21. For more on inclusion you might see Hornby (2014); Imray and Colley (2017); Kauffman, Anastasiou, Badar, and Hallenbeck (in press); Gliona, Gonzales, and Jacobson (2005); Kauffman and Hallahan (1993, 1997, 2005); Kauffman, Ward, and Badar (2016); Warnock (2005).
22. Hall (2002, p. 148). See also Imray and Colley (2017), Kauffman, Felder, Ahrbeck, Badar, and Schneiders (in press).
23. For example, Worth (1999) wrote that special education is a scandal that "wastes money and hurts the poor" and is "the road to hell." Fisher (2001) wrote that "Special-ed is the gold-plated garbage can of American schooling." Cottle (2001) described special education as "a disaster" that is "poorly defined, poorly run, poorly enforced." Cook and Schirmer (2006) noted similar denigrations of special education and found it necessary to publish

what is special about it. Bateman, Lloyd, and Tankersley (2015) included a chapter on why special education is needed. Kauffman, Anastasiou, and Maag (2017) described special education as facing an identity crisis, in part because of severe criticism even from individuals practicing the profession.

24. Walker (2003).
25. Kauffman and Anastasiou (in press).
26. Imray and Colley (2017); Kauffman and Hallahan (2005).
27. For more on prevention, see Kauffman (1999, 2014) and Kauffman and Badar (2018).
28. Martin (2013) provides perspective on why federal legislation was necessary in the case of special education. Yell et al. (2017) describe the evolution of federal law. Returning responsibility for special education to states would involve devolution, in our opinion. Cannon, Gregory, and Waterstone (2013) recommend focusing on the framework of IDEA. Anastasiou, Gregory, and Kauffman (in press) evaluate inclusion as a matter of international law.

References

Algozzine, B., Christenson, S., & Ysseldyke, J. E. (1982). Probabilities associated with the referral to placement process. *Teacher Education and Special Education, 5*(3), 19–23.

Anastasiou, D., Gregory, M., & Kauffman, J. M. (in press). Commentary on Article 24 of the CRPD: The right to education. In I. Bantekas, M. Stein, & D. Anastasiou (Eds.), *Commentary on the UN Convention on the Rights of Persons with Disabilities.* New York, NY: Oxford University Press.

Anastasiou, D., Morgan, P. L., Farkas, G., & Wiley, A. L. (2017). Minority disproportionate representation in special education: Politics and evidence, issues and implications. In J. M. Kauffman, D. P. Hallahan, & P. C. Pullen (Eds.), *Handbook of special education* (2nd ed.). New York, NY: Routledge.

Bateman, B. D. (1994). Who, how, and where: Special education's issues in perpetuity. *The Journal of Special Education, 27,* 509–520.

Bateman, B. D. (2004). *Elements of successful teaching: General and special education students.* Verona, WI: IEP Resources.

Bateman, B. D. (2007). Law and the conceptual foundations of special education practice. In J. B. Crockett, M. M., Gerber, & T. J., & Landrum (Eds.), *Achieving the radical reform of special education: Essays in honor of James M. Kauffman* (pp. 95–114). Mahwah, NJ: Lawrence Erlbaum Associates.

Bateman, B. D. (2017). Individual education programs for children with disabilities. In J. M. Kauffman, D. P. Hallahan, & P. C. Pullen (Eds.), *Handbook of special education* (2nd ed., pp. 87–104). New York, NY: Routledge.

Bateman, B. D., & Linden, M. A. (2012). *Better IEPs: How to develop legally correct and educationally useful programs* (5th ed.). Verona, WI: Attainment.

Bateman, B. D., Lloyd, J. W., & Tankersley, M. (Eds.). (2015). *Enduring issues in special education: Personal perspectives.* New York, NY: Routledge.

Berninger, V. W., Abbott, R. D., Vermeulen, K., Ogier, S., Brooksher, R., Zook, D., & Lemos, Z. (2002). Comparison of faster and slower responders to early intervention in reading: differentiating features of their language profiles. *Learning Disability Quarterly, 25*, 59–76.

Cannon, Y., Gregory, M., & Waterstone, J. (2013). A solution hiding in plain sight: Special education and better outcomes for students with social, emotional, and behavioral challenges. *Fordham Urban Law Journal, 41*, 403–497.

Carpenter, B., & Bovair, K. (1996). Learning with dignity: Educational opportunities for students with emotional and behavioral difficulties. *Canadian Journal of Special Education, 11*(1), 6–16.

Carr, M. R. (2004, January 4). My son's disability, and my own inability to see it. *Washington Post,* B5.

Centers for Disease Control and Prevention (2017). Vaccines do not cause autism. Retrieved May 6, 2017 from cdc.gov/vaccinesafety/concerns/autism.html

Cook, B. G., & Schirmer, B. R. (Eds.). (2006). *What's special about special education? Examining the role of evidence-based practices.* Austin, TX: PRO-ED.

Cottle, M. (2001, June 18). Jeffords kills special ed. reform school. *The New Republic,* 14–15.

Deno, E. (1970). Special education as developmental capital. *Exceptional Children, 37*, 229–237.

Edgerton, R. B. (1967). *The cloak of competence: Stigma in the lives of the mentally retarded.* Berkeley, CA: University of California Press.

Edgerton, R. B. (1993). *The cloak of competence* (revised and updated) Berkeley, CA: University of California Press.

Engelmann, S. (1997). Theory of mastery and acceleration. In J. W. Lloyd, E. J. Kameenui, & D. Chard (Eds.), *Issues in educating students with disabilities* (pp. 177–195). Mahwah, NJ: Erlbaum.

Feynman, R. P. (1985). *"Surely you're joking, Mr. Feynman!" Adventures of a curious character.* New York, NY: Norton.

Fisher, M. (2001, December 13). Students still taking the fall for D.C. schools. *The Washington Post*, B1, B4.

Forness, S. R., Freeman, S. F. N., Paparella, T., Kauffman, J. M., & Walker, H. M. (2012). Special education implications of point and cumulative prevalence for children with emotional or behavioral disorders. *Journal of Emotional and Behavioral Disorders, 20,* 1–14.

Forness, S. R., & Knitzer, J. (1992). A new proposed definition and terminology to replace "serious emotional disturbance" in Individuals with Disabilities Education Act. *School Psychology Review, 21,* 12–20.

Fuchs, D., & Fuchs, L. S. (1994). Inclusive schools movement and the radicalization of special education reform. *Exceptional Children, 60,* 294–309.

Fuchs, D., & Fuchs, L. S. (1995). What's "special" about special education? *Phi Delta Kappan, 76,* 522–530.

Fuchs, D., Fuchs, L. S., & Stecker, P. M. (2010). The "blurring" of special education in a new continuum of general education placements and services. *Exceptional Children, 76,* 301–323. doi: doi.org/10.1177/001440291007600304

Gerber, M. M. (2005). Teachers are still the test: Limitations of response to instruction strategies for identifying children with learning disabilities. *Journal of Learning Disabilities, 38,* 516–524.

Gerber, M. M. (2017). A history of special education. In J. M. Kauffman, D. P. Hallahan, & P., C. Pullen (Eds.), *Handbook of special education* (2nd ed., pp. 3–15). New York, NY: Routledge.

Gerber, M. M., & Semmel, M. I. (1984). Teacher as imperfect test: Reconceptualizing the referral process. *Educational Psychologist, 19,* 137–148.

Gliona, M. F., Gonzales, A. K., & Jacobson, E. S. (2005). Suggested changes in thinking about instructional environments and in the language of special education. In J. M. Kauffman & D. P. Hallahan (Eds.), *The illusion of full inclusion: A comprehensive critique of a current special education bandwagon* (2nd ed.). Austin, TX: PRO-ED.

Gordon, N. (2017, September 20). Race, poverty, and interpreting overrepresentation in special education. Washington, DC: Brookings Institution. Downloaded September 23, 2017 from https://www.brookings.edu/research/race-poverty-and-interpreting-overrepresentation-in-special-education/

Gould, S. J. (1996a). *Full house: The spread of excellence from Plato to Darwin*. New York, NY: Three Rivers Press.

Gould, S. J. (1996b). *The mismeasure of man* (revised & expanded ed.). New York, NY: Norton.

Gresham, F. M. (2002). Responsiveness to intervention: An alternative approach to the identification of learning disabilities. In R. Bradley, L. Danielson, & D. P. Hallahan (Eds.), *Identification of learning disabilities: Research to practice* (pp. 467–547). Mahwah, NJ: Lawrence Erlbaum Associates.

Hall, J. P. (2002). Narrowing the breach: Can disability culture and full educational inclusion be reconciled? *Journal of Disability Policy Studies, 13*, 144–152.

Hallahan, D. P., Kauffman, J. M., & Pullen, P. C. (2018). *Exceptional learners: Introduction to special education* (14th ed.). Upper Saddle River, NJ: Pearson.

Hallahan, D. P., Lloyd, J. W., Kauffman, J. M., Weiss, M., & Martinez, E. (2005). *Introduction to learning disabilities* (3rd ed.). Boston, MA: Allyn & Bacon.

Hallahan, D. P., & Mercer, C. D. (2002). Learning disabilities: Historical perspectives. In R. Bradley, L. Danielson, & D. P. Hallahan (Eds.). *Identification in learning disabilities: Research to practice* (pp. 1–67). Mahwah, NJ: Lawrence Erlbaum Associates.

Hanushek, E. A., Kain, J. F., & Rivkin, S. G. (2002). Inferring program effects for special populations: Does special education raise achievement for students with disabilities? *Review of Economics and Statistics, 84*, 584–599.

Helderman, R. S. (2003, October 6). Va. Tries to balance its needs: Budget shortfall threatens to consolidate sister schools for the deaf and blind. *Washington Post*, B1, B7.

Hendrick, I. G., & MacMillan, D. L. (1989). Selecting children for special education in New York City: William Maxwell, Elizabeth Farrell, and the development of ungraded classes, 1900–1920. *The Journal of Special Education, 22*, 395–417.

Heward, W. L. (2003). Ten faulty notions about teaching and learning that hinder the effectiveness of special education. *The Journal of Special Education, 36*, 186–205.

Horn, J. L. (1924). *The education of exceptional children: A consideration of public school problems and policies in the field of differential education*. New York, NY: Century.

Hornby, G. (2014). *Inclusive special education: Evidence-based practices for children with special needs and disabilities*. New York, NY: Springer.

Huefner, D. S. (2006). *Getting comfortable with special education law: A framework for working with children with disabilities* (2nd ed.). Norwood, MA: Christopher Gordon.

Huefner, D. S. (2015). Placements for special education students: The promise and the peril. In B. D. Bateman, J. W. Lloyd, & M. Tankersley (Eds.), *Enduring issues in special education: Personal perspectives* (pp. 215–230). New York, NY: Routledge.

Imray, P., & Colley, A. (2017). *Inclusion is dead: Long live inclusion.* New York, NY: Routledge.

Jacobson, J. W., Foxx, R. M., & Mulick, J. A. (2016). Facilitated communication: The ultimate fad treatment. In R. M. Foxx & J. A. Mulick (Eds.), *Controversial therapies for autism and intellectual disabilities: Fad, fashion, and science in professional practice* (2nd ed., pp. 283–302). New York, NY: Routledge.

Kauffman, J. M. (1976). Nineteenth century views of children's behavior disorders: Historical contributions and continuing issues. *The Journal of Special Education, 10,* 335–349. doi: 10.1177/002246697601000 402

Kauffman, J. M. (1981). Introduction: Historical trends and contemporary issues in special education in the United States. In J. M. Kauffman & D. P. Hallahan (Eds.), *Handbook of special education* (pp. 3–23). Englewood Cliffs, NJ: Prentice-Hall.

Kauffman, J. M. (1983). From the editor: On the missing millions. *Exceptional Education Quarterly, 3*(4), vii–ix.

Kauffman, J. M. (1999). How we prevent the prevention of emotional and behavioral disorders. *Exceptional Children, 65,* 448–468.

Kauffman, J. M. (1999–2000). The special education story: Obituary, accident report, conversion experience, reincarnation, or none of the above? *Exceptionality, 8*(1), 61–71. doi: 10.1207/S15327035EX080 1_6

Kauffman, J. M. (2003). Appearances, stigma, and prevention. *Remedial and Special Education, 24,* 195–198. doi: 10.1177/074193250302 40040201

Kauffman, J. M. (2004). The president's commission and the devaluation of special education. *Education and Treatment of Children, 27,* 307–324.

Kauffman, J. M. (2005). Waving to Ray Charles: Missing the meaning of disability. *Phi Delta Kappan, 86,* 520–521, 524.

Kauffman, J. M. (2008). Would we recognize progress if we saw it? A commentary. *Journal of Behavioral Education, 17,* 128–143. doi: 10.1007/s10864-007-9060-z

Kauffman, J. M. (2010). *The tragicomedy of public education: Laughing and crying, thinking and fixing*. Verona, WI: Attainment.

Kauffman, J. M. (2011). *Toward a science of education: The battle between rogue and real science*. Verona, WI: Attainment.

Kauffman, J. M. (2014). How we prevent the prevention of emotional and behavioral difficulties in education. In P. Garner, J. Kauffman, & J. G. Elliott (Eds.), *The Sage handbook of emotional and behavioral difficulties in education* (2nd ed.). London: Sage.

Kauffman, J. M. (2015a). The "B" in EBD is not just for bullying. *Journal of Research in Special Educational Needs, 15*, 167–175. doi: 10.1111/1471-3802.121021

Kauffman, J. M. (2015b). Opinion on recent developments and the future of special education. *Remedial and Special Education, 36*, 9–13. doi: 10.1177/0741932514543653

Kauffman, J. M. (2015c). Why exceptionality is more important for special education than exceptional children. *Exceptionality, 25*, 225–236. doi: 10.1080/09362835.2014.986609

Kauffman, J. M. (2015d). Why we should have special education. In B. Bateman, J. Lloyd, & M. Tankersley (Eds.), *Enduring issues in special education: Personal perspectives* (pp. 397–408). New York, NY: Routledge.

Kauffman, J. M., & Anastasiou, D. (in press). On cultural politics in special education: Is much of it justifiable? *Journal of Disability Policy Studies*.

Kauffman, J. M., Anastasiou, D., Badar, J., & Hallenbeck, B. A. (in press). Becoming your own worse enemy: Converging paths. In C. Boyle, S. Mavropoulou, J. Anderson, & A. Page (Eds.), *Inclusive education: Global issues & controversies*. Rotterdam, Netherlands: SENSE.

Kauffman, J. M., Anastasiou, D., Badar, J., Travers, T. C., & Wiley, A. L. (2016). Inclusive education moving forward. In J. P. Bakken & F. E. Obiakor, (Eds.), *Advances in special education, Vol. 32— General and special education in an age of change: Roles of professionals involved* (pp. 153–177). Bingley, UK: Emerald.

Kauffman, J. M., Anastasiou, D., & Maag, J. W. (2017). Special education at the crossroad: An identity crisis and the need for a scientific reconstruction. *Exceptionality, 25*, 139–155.

Kauffman, J. M., & Badar, J. (2013). How we might make special education for students with emotional or behavioral disorders less stigmatizing. *Behavioral Disorders, 39*, 16–27.

Kauffman, J. M., & Badar, J. (2014a). Better thinking and clearer communication will help special education. *Exceptionality, 22*, 17–32. doi: 10.1080/09362835.2014.865953

Kauffman, J. M., & Badar, J. (2014b). Instruction, not inclusion, should be the central issue in special education: An alternative view from the USA. *Journal of International Special Needs Education, 17*, 13–20.

Kauffman, J. M., & Badar, J. (2016). It's instruction over place(not the other way around! *Phi Delta Kappan, 98*(4), 55–59. doi: 10.1177/0031721716681778

Kauffman, J. M., & Badar, J. (2017). Extremism and disability chic. *Exceptionality, 26*, 46–61.

Kauffman, J., & Badar, J. (2018). *The scandalous neglect of children's mental health needs: What schools can do.* New York, NY: Routledge.

Kauffman, J. M., Badar, J., & Wiley, A. L. (in press). RtI: Controversies and solutions. In P. C. Pullen & M. M. Kennedy (Eds.), *Handbook of response to intervention and multi-tiered systems of support.* New York, NY: Routledge.

Kauffman, J. M., Bantz, J., & McCullough, J. (2002). Separate and better: A special public school class for students with emotional and behavioral disorders. *Exceptionality, 10*, 149–170.

Kauffman, J. M., Bruce, A., & Lloyd, J. W. (2012). Response to intervention (RtI) and students with EBD. In J. P. Bakken, F. E. Obiakor, & A. Rotatori (Eds.), *Advances in special education, Vol. 23—Behavioral disorders: Current perspectives and issues* (pp. 107–127). Bingley, UK: Emerald.

Kauffman, J. M., Felder, M., Ahrbeck, B., Badar, J., & Schneiders, K. (in press). Inclusion of *all* students in general education? International appeal for a more temperate approach to inclusion, *Journal of International Special Needs Education.*

Kauffman, J. M., & Hallahan, D. P. (1993). Toward a comprehensive delivery system for special education. In J. I. Goodlad & T. C. Lovitt (Eds.), *Integrating general and special education* (pp. 73–102). Columbus, OH: Merrill/Macmillan.

Kauffman, J. M., & Hallahan, D. P. (1997). A diversity of restrictive environments: Placement as a problem of social ecology. In J. W. Lloyd, E. J. Kameenui, & D. Chard (Eds.), *Issues in educating students with disabilities* (pp. 325–342). Hillsdale, NJ: Erlbaum.

Kauffman, J. M., & Hallahan, D. P. (Eds.). (2005). *The illusion of full inclusion: A comprehensive critique of a current special education bandwagon* (2nd ed.). Austin, TX: PRO-ED.

Kauffman, J. M., & Landrum, T. J. (2006). *Children and youth with emotional and behavioral disorders: A history of their education.* Austin, TX: Pro-Ed.

Kauffman, J. M., & Landrum, T. J. (2007). Educational service interventions and reforms. In J. W. Jacobson, J. A. Mulick, & J. Rojahn (Eds.), *Handbook of intellectual and developmental disabilities* (pp. 173–188). New York, NY: Springer.

Kauffman, J. M., & Landrum, T. J. (2009). Politics, civil rights, and disproportional identification of students with emotional and behavioral disorders. *Exceptionality, 17*, 177–188. doi: 10.1080/09362830903231903

Kauffman, J. M., & Landrum, T. J. (2018). *Characteristics of emotional and behavioral disorders of children and youth* (11th ed.). Upper Saddle River, NJ: Prentice-Hall.

Kauffman, J. M., & Lloyd, J. W. (2017). Statistics, data, and special education decisions: Basic links to realities. In J. M. Kauffman, D. P. Hallahan, & P. C. Pullen (Eds.), *Handbook of special education* (2nd ed., pp. 29–39). New York, NY: Routledge.

Kauffman, J. M., Nelson, C. M., Simpson, R. L., & Ward, D. R. (2017). Contemporary issues. In In J. M. Kauffman, D. P. Hallahan, & P. C. Pullen (Eds.), *Handbook of special education* (2nd ed., pp. 16–28). New York, NY: Routledge.

Kauffman, J. M., & Pullen, P. L. (1996). Eight myths about special education. *Focus on Exceptional Children, 28*(5), 1–12.

Kauffman, J. M., Pullen, P. L., Mostert, M. P., & Trent, S. C. (2011). *Managing classroom behavior: A reflective case-based approach* (5th ed.) Upper Saddle River, NJ: Pearson.

Kauffman, J. M., Ward, D. M., & Badar, J. (2016). The delusion of full inclusion. In R. M. Foxx & J. A. Mulick (Eds.), *Controversial therapies for autism and developmental disabilities* (2nd ed). New York, NY: Routledge.

Kauffman, J. M., & Wiley, A. L. (2004). How the President's Commission on Excellence in Special Education (PCESE) devalues special education. *Learning Disabilities: A Multidisciplinary Journal, 13*, 3–6.

Kavale, K. A. (2002). Discrepancy models in the identification of learning disability. In R. Bradley, L. Danielson, & D. P. Hallahan (Eds.), *Identification of learning disabilities: Research to practice* (pp. 369–426). Mahwah, NJ: Lawrence Erlbaum Associates.

Landrum, T. J. (2015). Science matters in special education. In B. Bateman, J. W. Lloyd, & M. Tankersley (Eds.), *Enduring issues in special education: Personal perspectives* (pp. 429–440). New York, NY: Routledge

Landrum, T. J., & Tankersley, M. (2004). Science in the schoolhouse: An uninvited guest. *Journal of Learning Disabilities, 37*, 207–212.

Letter. (2015, October 23). Dear Colleagues letter from Michael K. Yudin, U.S. Dept. of Education, Office of Special Education and Rehabilitative Services.

Lloyd, J. W., Repp, A. C., & Singh, N. N. (Eds.) (1991). *The regular education initiative: Alternative perspectives on concepts, issues, and methods.* Dekalb, IL: Sycamore.

Lynch, R. (2004). *Exceptional returns: Economic, fiscal and social benefits of investment in early childhood development.* Washington, DC: Economic Policy Institute.

MacMillan, D. L., & Hendrick, I. G. (1993). Evolution and legacies. In J. I. Goodlad & T. C. Lovitt (Eds.), *Integrating general and special education.* Columbus, OH: Merrill/Macmillan.

Maag, J. W., Kauffman, J. M., & Simpson, R. L. (2018). The amalgamation of special education? On practices and policies that may render it unrecognizable. *Exceptionality.* Published online February 5, 2018, doi: doi.org/10.1080/09362835.2018.1425624

Mann, L. (1979). *On the trail of process: A historical perspective on cognitive processes and their training.* New York, NY: Grune & Stratton.

Martin, E. W. (1974). Some thoughts on mainstreaming. *Exceptional Children, 41*, 150–153.

Martin, E. W. (2013). *Breakthrough: Federal special education legislation 1965–1981.* Sarasota, FL: Bardolf.

Martin, E. W. Jr. (2017, May 7). Motivated by Bev's comment on defense of EAHCA/IDEA. Email to spedpro@virginia.edu.

Mattison, R. E. (2014). The interface between child psychiatry and special education in the treatment of students with emotional/behavioral disorders in school settings. In H. M. Walker & F. M. Gresham (Eds.), *Handbook of evidence-based practices for emotional and behavioral disorders: Applications in schools* (pp. 104–126). New York, NY: Guilford.

Memorandum. (2008, July 28). To chief state school officers, state directors of special education, from William W. Knudsen, Acting Director, Office of Special Education Programs, U.S. Department of Education.

Mez, J., McKee, A. C. et al. (2017). Clinicopathological evaluation of chronic traumatic encephalopathy in players of American football. *Journal of the American Medical Association, 318*, 360–370. doi: 10.1001/jama.2017.8334

Morgan, P. L., Farkas, G., Cook, M., Strassfeld, N. M., Hillemeier, M. M., Pun, W. H., & Schussler, D. L. (2016). Are black children disproportionately overrepresented in special education? A best-evidence synthesis. Exceptional Children, *83*, 1–18.

Mostert, M. P. (2014). An activist approach to debunking FC. *Research and Practice for Persons with Severe Disabilities, 39*, 203–210.

National Research Council (2002). *Minority students in special and gifted education.* Committee on Minority Representation in Special Education. M. S. Donovan & C. T. Cross (Eds.). Division of Behavioral and Social Sciences Education. Washington, DC: National Academy Press.

Popham, J. W. (2000). *Modern educational measurement: Practical guides for educational leaders* (3rd ed.). Boston, MA: Allyn & Bacon.

Presidents Commission on Excellence in Special Education. (2002). *A New Era: Revitalizing Special Education for Children and their Families.* Available at www.ed.gov/inits/commissionsboards/whspecialeducation/index.html. Washington, DC: U.S. Department of Education.

Pullen, P. C., & Hallahan, D. P. (2015). What is special education instruction? In B Bateman, J. W. Lloyd, & M. Tankersley (Eds.), *Enduring issues in special education: Personal perspectives* (pp. 37–50). New York, NY: Routledge.

Pullen, P. C., & Kennedy, M. M. (Eds.) (in press). *Handbook of response to intervention and multi-tiered systems of support.* New York, NY: Routledge.

Rhode, G., Jenson, W. R., & Reavis, H. K. (2010). *The tough kid book: Practical classroom management strategies* (2nd ed.). Eugene, OR: Pacific Northwest Publishing.

Rosenthal, B. M. (2016). HISD's focus on "over-identification" of black students backfires. Downloaded December 29, 2016 from www.houstonchronicle.com/news/houston-texas/houston/article/HISD-s-focus-on-over-identification-of-10821607.php?t=feb29e3481

Rosenthal, B. M., & Barned-Smith, S. J. (2016). Denied: Houston schools systematically block disabled kids from special ed. Downloaded December 29, 2016 from www.houstonchronicle.com/denied/6/

Sailor, W. S. (2009). *Making RTI work: How smart schools are reforming education through schoolwide Response-to-Intervention.* San Francisco, CA: Jossey-Bass & Wiley.

Sailor, W., & McCart, A. (2014). Stars in alignment. *Research and Practice for Persons with Severe Disabilities, 39*(1), 55–64.

Samuels, C. (2017, August 28). Minority students still missing out on special education, new analysis says. *Education Week.* Downloaded October 12, 2017 from http://blogs.edweek.org/edweek/speced/2017/08/minorities_underenrolled_special_education.html?utm_source=feedblitz&utm_medium=FeedBlitzRss&utm_campaign=onspecial education

Sanchez, A. L., Comacchio, D., Poznanski, B., Golik, A. M., Chou, T., & Comer, J. S. (2018).The effectiveness of school-based mental health services for elementary-aged children: A meta-analysis. *Journal of the American Academy of Child & Adolescent Psychiatry, 57*(3), 153–165.

Sarason, S. B., & Doris, J. (1979). *Educational handicap, public policy, and social history.* New York, NY: Macmillan.

Sasso, G. M. (2001). The retreat from inquiry and knowledge in special education. *The Journal of Special Education, 34,* 178–193.

Silvestri, S. M., & Heward, H. L. (2016). The neutralization of special education, revisited. In R. M. Foxx & J. A. Mulick (Eds.), *Controversial therapies for autism and intellectual disabilities: Fad, fashion, and science in professional practice* (2nd ed., pp. 136–153). New York, NY: Routledge.

Singer, J. D. (1988). Should special education merge with regular education? *Educational Policy, 2,* 409–424.

Spurlock, K. (2017, October 1). The right to read: My dyslexic daughter received years of tutoring and support. All children deserve such resources. *Washington Post Magazine,* 20–25. See also https://www.washingtonpost.com/lifestyle/magazine/years-of-tutoring-helped-my-dyslexic-daughter-read-all-kids-deserve-such-support/2017/09/27/60a81e6a-9405-11e7-89fa-bb822a46da5b_story.html?utm_term=.daf3a605f79f

Travers, J. C., Tincani, M. J., & Lang, R. (2015). Facilitated communication denies people with disabilities their voice. *Research and Practice for Persons with Severe Disabilities, 39,* 195–202.

U.S. Department of Education. (2002). *Twenty-fourth annual report to Congress on implementation of the Individuals with Disabilities Education Act.* Washington, DC: Author.

U.S. Department of Education. (2018). *Building the legacy: IDEA 2004.* Downloaded January 5, 2018 from http://idea.ed.gov/explore/view/p/,root,regs,300,B,300.115,.html

Vaughn, S., & Fuchs, L. S. (Eds.). (2003). Redefining learning disabilities as inadequate response to instruction. *Learning Disabilities Research and Practice, 18*(3) [special issue].

Walker, H. M. (2003, February 20). *Comments on accepting the Outstanding Leadership Award from the Midwest Symposium for Leadership in Behavior Disorders.* Kansas City, KS: Author.

Warnock, M. (2005). *Special educational needs: A new look. Impact No. 11.* London: Philosophy of Education Society of Great Britain.

Weintraub, F. J. (2012). A half century of special education: What we have achieved and the challenges we face. *Teaching Exceptional Children, 45,* 50–53.

Worth, R. (1999). The scandal of special-ed: It wastes money and hurts the poor. *The Washington Monthly, 31*(6).

Yell, M. L. (2015). *The law and special education* (4th ed.) Upper Saddle River, NJ: Pearson.

Yell, M. L., Katsiyannis, A., & Bradley, M. R. (2017). The Individuals with Disabilities Education Act: The evolution of special education law. In J. M. Kauffman, D. P. Hallahan, & P. C. Pullen (Eds.), *Handbook of special education* (2nd ed., pp. 55–70-). New York, NY: Routledge.

Zigmond, N. P. (1997). Educating students with disabilities: The future of special education. In J. W. Lloyd, E. J. Kameenui, & D. Chard (Eds.), *Issues in educating students with disabilities* (pp. 377–390). Mahwah, NJ: Erlbaum.

Zigmond, N. P. (2003). Where should students with disabilities receive special education services? Is one place better than another? *The Journal of Special Education, 37*, 193–199.

Zigmond, N. P., & Kloo, A. (2017). General and special education are (and should be) different. In J. M. Kauffman, D. P. Hallahan, & P., C. Pullen (Eds.), *Handbook of special education* (2nd ed., pp. 249–262). New York, NY: Routledge.

Index

Note: bold page numbers indicate tables; numbers preceded by 'n' are chapter endnote numbers.